Make It Happen

Brock—

I loved our conversations about music, people, philosophers, etc. I am so grateful that you were my H.E.F.Y. co-leader. Good times. I hope you get to live out all your plans. Make it Happen!

May angels guide your footsteps And God guide your heart

Make It Happen

A GUIDE TO HAPPINESS FOR LDS SINGLES

Kylee Shields, MSW

WALNUT SPRINGS PRESS

To my mom and dad

Walnut Springs Press, LLC
110 South 800 West
Brigham City, Utah 84302
walnutspringspress.blogspot.com

ISBN: 978-1-59992-870-8

ACKNOWLEDGMENTS

So many people have not only been a big part of this book but also my life. I am grateful for all my friends—their advice, words of wisdom, and challenges as I wrote this book. I appreciate the countless people with whom I've had enlightening conversations about life as a single Latter-day Saint. Thanks to the LP1 and LP2 Wards in Cambridge, Massachusetts, as well as the University Stake at Arizona State University, for their time and for letting me conduct focus groups with single members as research for this book.

Much of the inspiration for this book came from Master Mind, ANASAZI, INSPIRE, music nights, writing groups, singles wards, family wards, Brigham Young University football games at Grandma's house, and teaching seminary at Spanish Fork High School and early-morning seminary in Belmont, Massachusetts. I also want to give credit to Especially for Youth (EFY), BYU, the graduate school at Arizona State University, and AmeriCorps VISTA. In addition, I learned a great deal on my trips to Africa, Italy, Israel, Jerusalem, Scotland, and Ireland.

I have so many people to thank for helping this book become a reality, and especially for supporting me as I worked on it. Much thanks to my awesome editor Linda Prince and marketing director and designer Amy Orton, to Brandon Burnham for seeing that I was born to be a sailor, and to my lifelong best friend Kimberlee Ann Young Cook. Big thanks to Catherine Papworth, Jake Black, Kristen "Schoney" Lee, Jodi Cantrell, Alycesun Clare, Ron Bartholomew, Lori Lish, Timothy Connor, Joshua Boyle, Marcelo Gomes, Lincoln Pearce, Aaron Kitterman, Angie Whitman, Kris Gurr, Angela Eschler, Elona Shelley, Jamie Nelson, Alexis Solomon, Miranda Culver, Becky Martin, Kelly Nelson, Liz Shields, Hillary Clemens, K. Marie Criddle, Daniel

Woolston, William Cobb, Camille Whiting, Dani Shields Tvetan, and Chelsea Shields Strayer.

I appreciate my incredible, supportive family, especially my parents. Though they have no idea what it is like to be a "mid-single," they have the wisdom to let me share, the love to let me live, and the patience to see me through the tough days.

Most importantly, I need to acknowledge that God has been deeply in the details of this book.

Table of Contents

INTRODUCTION
So What?

Of course marriage is desirable; of course it is hoped for and worked for and sought after. But worrying about it will never bring it. In fact, it may have the opposite effect, for there is nothing that dulls a personality so much as a negative outlook. Possibly some of you will not be married; but don't forget that there are other things in life, other pursuits to be followed.

—GORDON B. HINCKLEY ("FORGET YOURSELF," 1977)

Recently, I went to a job interview, and the first question I was asked was "So, are you single, married, or divorced?" Surprised, I replied, "I'm single—very single." The interviewer laughed and said, "We will help you with that here." I smiled and said, "Great, then I'll take the job." I sat down and had one of my best job interviews ever. I learned that this nonprofit company, in addition to all the good they do with troubled adolescents, has had 250-plus marriages over the years with their employees (that's over 500 people). Who needs health insurance when you have those kind of benefits! I took the job, and I'm hoping they follow through as advertised.

In the mean time, if you are anything like me—single, very single—this book is for you. While some of the principles and ideas aren't specific to singles, I wrote the book for singles and from a single-adult perspective.

There is an infamous quote attributed to Brigham Young about guys that are single and twenty-five or older being a menace to society. I've never actually found that quote, but I have met plenty of "menaces" that are remarkable. I have associated with incredible LDS singles throughout the world, and each of them has lessons to teach and life to share. I have met people who have been single out of choice, single by divorce, single because of the death of a spouse, or single because they have simply never had the chance to marry. Being single and over the age of twenty-one used to be an anomaly in the Church, but these days there are entire stakes full of single adults. Over the past thirteen years, I have been a member of singles wards in four different states and several foreign countries. I love being single and being a member of the LDS Church. Don't get me wrong. I would love to be married and have children—this is my heart's desire—but so far this has not been my reality.

When I moved to Boston as a twenty-six-year-old single, I didn't know a soul, and I instantly fell in love with New England and all it had to offer. I enjoyed being a part of the singles ward in Cambridge, which was full of brilliant single adults. I met singles who were bitter, lonely, or waiting around for someone to rescue them, as well as ambitious singles who worked sixty to eighty hours a week and flew across the world for meetings, trying to climb the ladder of success. I was in awe and found myself a bit lost. I wasn't bitter about being single, yet I wasn't launching an amazing career that filled my days and nights. I was somewhere in between.

The more I talked with other singles, the more I realized the difficulty of navigating through life as an older single Mormon. I remember thinking that at some point, maybe age thirty or so, I could let go of my dreams of being married and having kids. Ha! Wouldn't it be great if at a certain age the Lord would just let us know if we would be getting married in the future or not? Then we could plan accordingly. Those who were never going to get married could stop dragging themselves on endless blind dates, setups, and single mix and mingles. Those who were eventually going to get married would try harder at the flirting thing or the asking-out thing. Unfortunately, this just doesn't happen. As a result, single adults get tired and frustrated in a religious culture that caters to families. You feel like you are a square peg trying desperately to fit into a round hole.

With all this in mind, and knowing there are so many others like me out there, I started to blog and write about different principles or ideas that helped me and others to be happy. Throughout the writing process, one thing has remained constant. I know the Lord knows and loves every one of His children. He knows about all the single adults out there in the Church, and He loves them. He hears the pleas of their parents. He knows the deep, dark loneliness that accompanies a single life. He is aware of broken dreams and plans that don't make sense. He understands the incredible joy of getting married and then the incomprehensible pain and loneliness of getting divorced or being widowed. He knows about arms that ache to hold children, wedding plans and cuttings from magazines that sit in a file somewhere, and savings accounts set up to buy a wedding ring. He understands biological clocks and cultural pressure, and He knows if you really are too picky or not. He knows *you.* He wants you to not only be happy in the life to come, but also in this life. So I issue you a challenge. *What are you going to do with your single life?* How are you going to build the kingdom in your own unique way? What are you going to contribute that no one else can or will? You may be single, but so what?

Years ago I was sitting in a seminary class where my teacher had decided not to talk at all during class. Instead he held up large index cards to help us teach each other the lesson. He wrote the block of scripture for the lesson on the board and then turned the class over to us. If we were on topic, he would hold up a card that said, "Keep going," or "What is that scripture saying?" If we were going astray or not picking out the right principles, the teacher would hold up cards that said, "Stop," or "Look closer." I don't remember much about those silent lessons, but I remember that my favorite index card said, "So what?" My teacher loved to say this during class. It wasn't enough to just talk about the lesson or the principle. The most important part of the lesson was when we applied the lessons to our own lives. If we didn't apply the principles to our lives, they were just words. The "so what?" part of my classes are what have stuck with me after all these years.

So, what are you going to do to make things happen in your single life? What does it mean to be happy and single? What does it mean to be successful and single? Whoever you are, you are keenly aware of the circumstances that brought you to open this book.

I don't claim to be any kind of expert when it comes to being single, but I *am* single, so I know what it feels like. This book is a collection of ideas, blog posts I've written, lessons I've learned, informal discussions I've had with incredible and ordinary people on couches and floors, and experiences that have helped me to be a healthy, happy, single person.

If you are stuck in your life and wondering where to find inspiration, if you need some variety in your routine, if your scripture studying needs a change-up, if fear is ousting your faith, I hope you can find some answers in this book. You will also find sections dealing with loss, trials, learning to be present, making things happen, being still, disconnecting from the world and technology, and learning how to be grateful. You will learn how to work on your relationships; how to set, keep, and make your goals come to life; how to listen and validate; and most importantly, how to love yourself. I hope you will find the principles that work for you, and go apply them in your life.

ONE
Dating—Or the Lack Thereof

If you are just marking time waiting for a marriage prospect,
stop waiting. You may never have the opportunity for a suitable
marriage in this life, so stop waiting and start moving.
Prepare yourself for life—even a single life—by education,
experience, and planning. Don't wait for happiness to
be thrust upon you. Seek it out in service and learning.
Make a life for yourself. And Trust in the Lord.
—DALLIN H. OAKS ("DATING VERSUS HANGING OUT," 2005)

The other day at church I was sitting with a family, waiting
for sacrament meeting to begin, when the three-year-old sitting
next to me asked, "Why did you come to church with her?" She
was pointing to my roommate, so I explained that I live with
three girls. The toddler looked very confused and asked, "Well,
why don't you have husbands?" I laughed at her confusion and
curiosity and smiled. It was a good question. Her mother was
completely embarrassed and apologized multiple times on her
daughter's behalf.

I'm sure you've had similar experiences—some are kinder
than others. The first thing people asked me when they learned

15

I was writing a book about being single was if there would be a chapter about dating. I found this funny, since I am obviously not a pro in the dating field. However, you don't get to be a thirty-two-year-old LDS single without at least a few eclectic dating experiences. For example, one time my date forgot his wallet and was asked to leave something for collateral while he retrieved it. Guess what he left for collateral? Yep, he left me. I sat there for about forty-five minutes while he drove to who-knows-where to get his wallet. I am sure you've had your fair share of dating drama.

I don't really understand the dating process. If I knew how to date, or be in a perfect relationship, I probably wouldn't be writing this book about being single. I am one of those girls who collects guy friends by the dozens but can't seem to keep a boyfriend around very long. I have had my fair share of awful dates—and good ones, too. I've received all kinds of dating advice, from "Be yourself" to "Don't be yourself so much." I've had plenty of setups and blind dates. I've also heard other people's stories of dating horrors, as well as magical dating moments where miracles happen and two people actually hit it off.

When you say the word *dating* to anyone who's been single for a while, it can evoke many different emotions. It often brings up a conversation about what kind of guy or girl you are looking for. I find myself fascinated with these discussions. Some people are very particular, while others don't seem to know what they want. I've noticed that over time, these conversations have changed a lot. When I was younger, the dating process often involved a lot of lists. Girls made lists of the attributes they wanted in a guy, and guys had lists of what they wanted in a girl. As I got older, it seemed people's lists changed, became shorter, or were completely thrown out. I realized I needed to come up with an answer when people asked me what kind of a guy I wanted to date. Since I had never really made a list, I thought a lot about the attributes I wanted in a guy and came up with a simple answer. Now whenever someone asks me what kind of guy I want to date, I tell them I want a KB.

KB

Working with youth in many capacities, I always get asked if I'm married, dating, etc. One day at work a girl asked me, "Miss Kylee, are you a mom?" When I said no, she said, "Well, you look like you could be a mom." I laughed. Typically when I say no, people ask what kind of a guy I am looking for. Years ago I honed in on a perfect and succinct answer for the curious people in my life. It is still what I say to this day. I tell them, "I'm looking for a KB." Naturally they want to know what a KB is, and that is when I get to tell them, Mormon or not, that I'm looking for a kingdom builder.

Many people understand this idea. When they don't understand, I usually say I'm looking for someone who is running in life, working on goals, and building others along the way, and someone who puts God first. I learned long ago not to make a list of qualities of the "perfect" guy for me. I have met guys who have completely changed my opinion on things I thought I was solid about. I have also met guys who have introduced me to ideas I never even knew existed. The more people I meet, the more passionate I become about dating someone who is a KB.

THE EVOLUTION OF DATING

In my lifetime, dating has changed dramatically. I remember the days when guys actually asked girls out on dates—the whole planned, paired-off, and paid-for kind. I remember it not being that big of a deal—it was something you just did. I loved going on lots of different dates with different guys my first few years of college. Then things started to change. Enter the "hang-out" phase of dating. There was a dramatic shift from one-on-one dating to hanging out in groups.

One day, I told a guy friend that I didn't understand his form of dating. When I referred to it as "pre-dating," he looked at me in obvious confusion. I said I didn't understand why he would go to different group activities and basically pre-date a girl by watching how she interacted with others, seeing if she was funny and nice, etc. Then if she passed the test (after weeks or even months), he would ask her out. He smiled and agreed that is exactly how he "dates." I asked him how well it was working for him. We both laughed because he was as single as ever. I asked him if it wouldn't have just saved him time and energy if he had just asked her out on a date and found out, in one night, if he wanted to get to know her more or if she just wasn't the girl for him. I know a lot of people who pre-date, but the truth is, no matter how hard you try, you can't really get to know an individual in a group setting. You can learn a lot about the person, but you don't actually get to know him or her.

One day, my home teachers (I call them HTs) visited my roommates and me. They shared a great lesson and, as usual, asked us if there was anything they could do for us. I was in a silly and sarcastic mood and told them that we needed a lot more dating in our house. They laughed and asked a few questions about our current dating situations. They were surprised to hear of our lack of dating opportunities. They wished us well and were on their way. I didn't think much of it because while I really did want to date more, I was just joking, right? WRONG! The next day, one of my HTs came over with his roommate and asked for me to come downstairs to talk to him. I wasn't expecting him, but I went downstairs in my pajamas with my hair in a messy bun, and glasses on my face. Little did I know what was about to happen.

SEVEN DATES IN SEVEN DAYS

As soon as I sat down, my HT told me that he had come up with a plan he called "Seven Dates in Seven Days." He said he had arranged for seven different guys to take me out on a date the next week, each on a different night, starting with Sunday night. All I had to do was agree. Of course, I was completely surprised, but I couldn't say no because I had actually *asked* for this! I could see my HT was really excited about the plan, so I accepted. He explained that he had picked a variety of guys, of different ages and with different occupations, interests, and hobbies. All he had told them about me was that I was new in the area and needed to get to know some people and places. I didn't know what to think when my HT left, but I knew I had a big week ahead of me.

When Sunday arrived, I got a phone call from my first date, letting me know what time he would pick me up and what I should wear. This is how it went each day of the week. I didn't know any of the guys or what we would be doing until they picked me up. I had so much fun with each of the seven guys. I got to eat something new every night—it was a great introduction to local restaurants—and I was surprised that not one of my dates was the typical dinner and a movie. I went kayaking on the river, went to Dave & Busters, went to a ward activity, played games, ate amazing food, and had incredible conversations. Each night I laughed, smiled, and was treated with the utmost respect. I went out with two students, a handyman, a guy in law school, a guy in medical school, a State Farm agent, and a police officer.

Each night after my date, my HT would call to see how things went. All he really wanted to know was if I was treated well and had a good time. I couldn't help but laugh as I told him of my adventures. Because one of the guys couldn't make it, I ended up going on my last date with my HT, the instigator, and we had a blast.

From this experience, I learned that dating is crucial to getting to know someone. This is simple but true. One of my dates was a guy I'd seen at a few social gatherings, but I'd never noticed him. When he took me out, I learned he was very passionate about his job, and that he was funny and kind. He could relate to me on many different levels. He was much more attractive than I ever gave him credit for. I wouldn't have known any of these things about him if I hadn't gone out with him on a date, one-on-one. Because the dates were all setups or blind dates, there wasn't any pressure, so the guys and I could just be ourselves. I'd like to say I found my Romeo in one of the seven guys, but I didn't. What I did get was an opportunity to be myself in different situations with different guys. I put myself out there, and if one of them had been interested after our first date, I'm sure he would've felt comfortable asking me out again. People asked me all the time when working on this book if I had any dating tricks or new ideas. I don't, but I thought this idea—seven dates in seven days—was brilliant. As it stands I found a bunch of great new guy friends that opened me up to new places, people, and networking opportunities.

TECHNOLOGY HAS ATROPHIED BRAVERY

There is a lot to be said about the do's and don'ts of dating. Books like *He's Just Not That into You* and *The Rules* each have their own take on the wild world of dating. So here are a few dating ideas and tips I came up with.

One time, a friend of mine met a guy while eating at Costa Vida, decided to give him my phone number, and then came home all excited for me to go out with said guy. I was nervous that she gave my number to an almost complete stranger, but was up for meeting him. The next day, the guy texted me and explained who he was and that my friend had told him to get a hold of me. Note to all guys out there: Don't tell a girl you were told to call her or text her or check her out on Facebook. Once someone suggests you call a girl, make your own decision to contact her. After that, you're on your own.

Then the guy tried to have a long "conversation" with me via text messaging. Note: Do not have conversations via text. Text messages are meant to be short and concise. He pretty much asked me all the first-date questions via text, and I finally realized we were on a "text date." I couldn't wait for the conversation to end. After I didn't respond to his message very quickly, I think he got the point, because he sent me his full name with the request to add him as a friend on Facebook. Note: Don't tell someone to add you as a friend on FB. If you are interested in finding out more about them via FB (in other words, stalking them), get their full name and request them as a friend.

Somewhere along the line, technology has started to rob people of their bravery. Instead of actually getting up the gumption to ask someone out face to face, we now text, Facebook, or even use Twitter. Instead of breaking up or having a hard conversation with someone, we hope to be able to leave a voice message. While I'm not anti-technology, I think some things just need to be done properly and maybe even in person.

MAKING OTHERS' DECISIONS

When it comes to dating, I have watched many guys take it upon themselves to make decisions for others. Here are a few examples. Scenario one: A guy likes a girl and he gets up the nerve to ask her out. The girl says she already has plans. The guy takes that as a no and gives up all hope of going out with said girl. Scenario two: A guy likes a girl but knows she is really popular—in fact, he knows many other guys who like said girl. Without even asking her out, he convinces himself that she is not interested in him. He consoles himself with the idea that he doesn't like to compete for attention. Do either of these scenarios sound familiar to you—from either perspective?

Now, I know there are times when girls say they are "busy" but what they really mean to say is "I'm not interested." I am also aware of the fact that the popular girl, the one who has all the guys after her, really might not be interested in the guy in the scenario above. But sometimes when a girl says she is busy, she really *is* busy, and sometimes the popular girl isn't interested in any of the guys who are brave enough to ask her out. Sometimes all it takes is actually liking someone enough to do hard things—or in other words, not making decisions for them, or assuming you know what they want or what they are thinking.

Let me explain. In the first scenario, if the guy likes the girl enough, he will give her multiple opportunities to tell him yes or no. It might be hard for the guy to ask her out multiple times and get turned down, but it gives the girl the opportunity to either finally say she is not interested or to make some time for him in her schedule. Either way the guy asks and the girl is given the opportunity to make a decision. In scenario two, the guy has already made the decision for the popular girl. He has taken away her ability to either say she would like to go out with him or that she isn't interested. Either way, if he doesn't ask, the girl is never given that opportunity because he has already run through the whole scene and decided for both of them that she isn't interested. Then he consoles himself with what he decides—that she wasn't worth the competition.

Guys, have enough love for yourself to do the hard things. If you like her, give her the chance to let you know how she feels about you. Take a chance that the popular girl might actually *want* you to ask her out and that she's tired of getting asked out by the "competition." Girls, make your own decisions and be honest. When a guy asks you out and you are not interested, just let him know. You can only use the "busy" excuse so many times before you need to give him some credit for his tenacity and be honest. If you really are busy, tell him you are interested in going out another time. If you are the popular girl, step away from the adoring crowd long enough to give time and attention to the guys who might lack the confidence to ask you out.

To summarize, in dating it is imperative to not try to make other people's decisions.

HONESTY IS THE BEST POLICY

While I don't have any new magic ways to get someone to ask you out, or genius ways to ask someone out, I do have a pretty good game plan. Honesty really is the best policy. Whether we are talking about being honest with those we date or being honest with ourselves, it is critical.

One day as I was talking to a bunch of single adults, a guy shared some dating stories, and one of them stuck with me. He said one of his hardest breakups was also his most beneficial. He had been dating a girl for a while and really liked her, but something just wasn't clicking with them. When they sat down and had the Determine the Relationship (DTR) chat, she told him she didn't want to date him anymore. He was shocked and asked her why. Instead of her just saying something like "It's not you, it's me," or "You are great—I'm just not feeling it," she actually cared about him enough to tell him the truth. She let him know that in their relationship he seemed to care more about what he was feeling, what he wanted to talk about, the decisions he was making, and so forth, than he did about her. He rarely took the time to ask her questions, listen to her answers, or give her opportunities to make decisions. He was so worried about coming across as this intelligent guy and getting his ideas out that he didn't give her the chance to share anything about herself.

As she explained why she no longer wanted to date him, he was shocked and automatically felt the need to be on the defense. He quickly finished the conversation, and the girl left. He told this group of single adults that right after she shut the door, he felt the Spirit strongly confirm to him that what she had said was true and that he needed to change.

While it was an awesome experience for him and he received feedback for his future dating experiences, I was amazed at the courage of the girl in the story. She took an opportunity—hard and awkward as it must have been—to be honest. As a result, this guy was able to really look at himself from a different perspective and make some needed changes. I remember him telling us that he was pretty sure he'd had that same problem in all his dating experiences before this girl, and he wondered why no one else had told him.

We all know why none of his earlier girlfriends told him. It was easier for them to just cut and run from the relationship than to actually sit there, look into his eyes, and love him enough to tell him hard things. And yet, it was those hard things that may have been holding him back all those years from having a great relationship. To hear his side is a bit sad. He told us that he used his intellectual conversations to compensate for his nervousness. Instead of maybe having to sit in awkward silence, he would just barrel through and fill up the space. Since this girl shared her feelings about their relationship, he said he has been learning to listen and sometimes sit in silence. He is applying the principle "Seek to understand before being understood" in his life, and he is learning how to be himself around the ladies.

So, whether you are looking for a KB, figuring out how to navigate the dating world, deciding if you should ask her out on Facebook or call her up, trying to come up with different ways to date, just getting back into the dating scene, or wishing you could just be done with dating all together, one thing is for sure—dating can be complicated and hard, but it can also be fun and amazing.

Action Questions

- Who are the KB's in your life? Why aren't you dating them?
- What is one goal you can set to increase your dating?
- How can you be more honest in dating (with others and with yourself), even if it's difficult?
- What are things you wished past boyfriends/girlfriends would have told you?
- How can you be okay when others use their agency and choose not to date you?

TWO
Hurricanes and Bridges

The people in our lives were placed there not only for us to enjoy but also to cross us and to dissatisfy us from time to time so that we can learn that love is not a matter of personal satisfaction but a going out of our hearts to empathize with, to understand, and to try to bless the other . . . to love the other, to forgive the other, to cease to demand that the other satisfy us, and to seek to be able to bless that person. Relationships were given to us to develop us in love.
—M. CATHERINE THOMAS *(SPIRITUAL LIGHTENING,* 1996)

We all have many types of relationships. You can't really live in this world without interacting with others—friends, roommates, coworkers, classmates, family, etc. This chapter will focus on two different types of relationships. I call them "hurricanes," or toxic relationships, and "bridges," or healthy relationships.

HURRICANES
Here are some signs that you are in a toxic relationship.
- When you are with that person, you find yourself constantly thinking negatively of yourself, or thinking about past situations or experiences with this person.

27

- On one or both person's part, there is much more talking than there is listening and exploring.
- When you are away from that person, all you think about is him or her (obsession).
- The relationship lacks validation, edification, and inspiration.

In one of my grad school internships, I worked as a therapist at a domestic violence (DV) shelter for victims of DV and for children who have witnessed it. I met with many women and a few children, on an individual and group basis. It was hard to see these women come into the shelter with broken jaws, swollen eyes, cuts, bruises all over their bodies, and more. It was even more difficult to see them enter the shelter with their children. When I first started the internship, I figured it would be hard to stay unbiased regarding the men who were abusing these women, but I soon found that wasn't the hardest part of my job. The hardest part was talking to women about their abusive relationships, gaining their trust, helping them learn how to be in healthy relationships in the future, and then watching many of them leave the shelter to return to their abusers. Time and time again I was shocked that these broken and beaten women would choose to return to an abusive situation.

One day, a client was telling me about her abuser. This was the third time she had left him, and she asked me whether or not she should go back to him. As you can imagine, I was frustrated and trying to figure out a way to help her. We had already talked about the abuse cycle of violence, power, and control, as well as many other issues that are typical in a toxic relationship.

I knew from some group sessions that this woman was very visual and liked stories, analogies, and pictures. Finally, an idea came to me. I asked her to picture her relationship in terms of a hurricane. I told her to picture herself and her abuser in the eye of the storm. In the eye of the storm, there is calm and peace. This was when their relationship was good. It could last for a long time or a very short time, but it was calm and things went well. Then I told her to imagine herself walking out into the hurricane to get away from her abuser, who was still in the eye.

At this point my client actually grimaced, so I asked her how she felt. She said she would be injured and blown away in the storm. Then I asked her how she could get out of the storm. I wasn't surprised when she said she should go back to the eye of the storm—back to her abuser. I asked her why she didn't think she could go *through* the storm to the other side, where there is no storm. She looked up at me and said she thought that would be too painful.

I acknowledged her pain and told her I agreed. To walk through the hurricane might mean she would be hit by some debris or struggle in the strong winds or rain, but once she got through the storm she would be safe. But she simply couldn't stay in the eye of the storm forever. I told her that getting out is sometimes painful, like being hit by the debris from a hurricane, because you miss what you are familiar with and you miss your abuser. But if this woman would endure the pain, work the program, and seek safety, she could weather the storm. If she waffled and stood too close to the hurricane, it would suck her back in, and she would run to the eye and back to her abuser. My client sat there silently for a moment, and I could tell something had finally clicked inside her. She looked up at me with tears in her eyes. She didn't want to be in the hurricane anymore!

I don't think relationships have to be as extreme as my client's abusive relationship to merit the title of hurricane. I am sure you have at least one friend who can't see that he or she is in a major storm in a dating relationship, but everyone else can see it. Your friend and his or her dating partner are on again, off again, and you are tired of hearing their troubles. You are starting to sound like a broken record when it comes to advice. It is hard to be friends with people who are in toxic relationships, because often they choose to stay in those relationships. They don't want to be alone, or they don't think they will survive the debris on their way out of the relationship. "Hurricane" relationships are toxic and destroy everything they touch. Because they are so volatile, you can see them from miles away.

BRIDGES

Here are some signs that you are in a healthy relationship.

- When you are with this person, you automatically think of ways to encourage, help, or inspire him or her.
- Being with this person is edifying, strengthening, empowering, and refreshing.
- Having this person in your life helps you to focus on the other things in your life (school, work, etc.).

- The relationship is one of growth and honesty.
- The relationship adds joy to your life and increases your sense of self-worth.

Most people know what a healthy relationship looks like. You could probably make a list of things you like about your positive relationships. You probably even know what a healthy relationship feels like. But do you know what makes one work? Do you know how you got into that amazing, healthy relationship in the first place? Those are much harder questions to answer. Healthy relationships take time, effort, and A LOT of work. They also take two people both working, at the same time, to succeed. It's much like building a bridge.

My only experience in building a bridge came back in high school. I participated in a bridge-building competition where teams were given supplies and had to build a bridge within a certain amount of time. Then, each bridge was tested to see how much weight it could hold. Sometimes in these competitions they use weights, and other times a person actually stands on the bridge to see if it can hold him or her. In our bridge competition, the bridges had to support weights that would be attached underneath. The bridge that could hold the most weight won the competition. Of course this activity had little to do with actually building bridges and more to do with making leaders and developing team-unity skills.

When we began the competition I knew very little about bridges. I knew they needed to be strong and create some kind of suspension, and that the two ends needed to be equal. I was grateful for my teammates who either knew a lot more about

31

building bridges or figured it out really quickly. We were given Popsicle-like sticks and glue. Right away one of my teammates told us that a triangle is the strongest shape, so I was given the job to make a bunch of triangles while the rest of the team figured out a game plan. I was happy to do my part. We knew we had to build evenly from each end so the bridge wouldn't fall. When both ends are built equally, they reach the middle at the same time and can be successfully attached to each other, causing a balance between the two ends. We didn't win the competition, although I thought we did a great job on our bridge. The thing I remember the most is one of my teammates telling us that no matter how great, beautiful, or powerful our bridge was, if it wasn't on a firm and even foundation, it would fail.

Successful bridges are built on firm foundations. Their integrity relies on an even footing. I'm sure you've seen the tragedy of a huge bridge collapsing due to shifting foundations during an earthquake. Engineers try to create bridges that will be flexible to shifting foundations, but in the end if the foundation is off, the integrity of the bridge suffers.

I think successful relationships are built in the same manner. Take a minute to think about the people in your life that you care about the most—the people you feel comfortable with, those with whom you can be yourself, and those that are refreshing to be around. Now think about the people in your life that you only want to be around only in small doses—the ones you keep at arm's length. What is the difference? One thing I've noticed is the way people build bridges with me. Those who take time to build a firm foundation, then equally give and take, create a strong and balanced relationship. The people in my life I struggle with are those with whom I continue to build up my side of the bridge, but they aren't doing their part. Eventually, I feel fatigued and drained by their unequal side, and my side of the bridge starts to collapse. Relationships that are only give or only take cannot withstand the earthquakes in life.

CHOOSE YOUR CIRCLE

Through the years I have formed many relationships, some bridges and some hurricanes. At one point, I realized I would give and give and give without expecting too much from people. This is exhausting! I found myself surrounded with friends who needed me but whom I couldn't rely on. I knew I needed to make some drastic changes, but the task seemed daunting. How do you surround yourself with happy, whole, successful, growing, enlightened people? How do you "cut out" the people who are sucking the life out of you? How do you stop building ineffective bridges, get out of the hurricanes, and create a new propinquity or circle of influence? The task is not easy, but it is well worth your time and effort.

For a good portion of my life, relationships just happened. I became friends with my coworkers, people I went to school with on a regular basis, and people from my ward. I didn't really pick and choose who my friends were—they just happened. If you are not actively seeking out positive, bridge-building relationships, you will be left with whatever relationships come your way. It took a while and quite a few hurricane-type friends for me to realize I can have much more control over the type of people I surround myself with.

As a social worker and therapist, I realized quickly that I needed to have people in my circle whom I could rely on. I needed to feel that once I was home from work I didn't need to be a therapist to my friends. I needed to have a positive support system to counteract my all-too-often-depressing job. So I started to seek out make-it-happen, positive people. I found myself making friends with them, wanting to be around them, and welcoming them into my circle. When I started doing this, something else changed inside me that I hadn't expected. I realized I had chosen my friends—actually handpicked them—and because of this I loved them that much more. I was willing to serve them and be there for them. They, in turn, treated me the same way. I am amazed at the difference it has made in my life since I started choosing my circle of friends and relationships instead of just letting them happen to me.

HURRICANE OR BRIDGE?

I've talked a lot in this chapter about recognizing hurricanes and bridges in your relationships, but what about you? Are you a hurricane or a bridge? Maybe you have been both at different times in your life. The key is to recognize which one you are in a particular situation, and then make changes accordingly.

Let's say you have a friend who is really struggling in life. He can't seem to find a job, is in and out of relationships (or can't seem to find *any* relationship), is lost without direction, and is crying out for help. It is as if he is drowning. When someone is drowning, he or she will usually scream out for help, thrash around, and grab whatever is nearby. And then the person starts to sink. As friends or family members, when we see someone drowning we want to help him or her. We don't want the person to struggle and be unhappy. We want him or her to be safe. We all want to help, but the difference is *how* we help.

Unfortunately, people who are hurricanes jump into the water and try to rescue the drowning person. When they do this, they are often hit or grabbed by the thrashing drowning person. If the would-be rescuer is pulled under the water, neither person is safe. Sometimes the water itself is toxic, and when you jump in to save the drowning person, you end up drowning too. I read a story about some kids that were playing outside in waist-high water. One of the kids walked too far out into the water where he could no longer touch the ground. He was drowning, so his three siblings and three cousins tried to save him by jumping into the water. None of them could swim. Someone witnessing the event saved the first child who fell in, but all of the other six kids drowned. It was tragic.

People who are bridge builders are aware of their surroundings and the complications that can occur when someone is drowning. Instead of jumping into the treacherous water or risking getting hurt by the drowning victim, the bridge builder stops and thinks. He or she looks at the surroundings and finds something to throw to the victim, creates a human chain, or tries to help the victim find safety. By staying on firm ground and coming up with solutions rather than adding to the problem, the bridge builder can better help the victim.

Many people are part hurricane and part bridge. It can be painful to walk away from a hurricane or choose to leave an unfinished or damaged bridge. But you will be so much happier in life if you build solid, firm bridges and stay away from hurricanes.

Action Questions

- How can you work through your negative thoughts about relationships?
- What things do you need in a healthy relationship?
- What can you do to build new relationships and strengthen existing ones?
- How do you "cut out" or let go of people who are sucking the life out of you?

THREE
Kigatsuku

*Kigatsuku means "an inner spirit to act without being told what
to do." When I was just a little girl, my mother began teaching
me to be kigatsuku. When she swept the floor, she would say,
"Chieko, what would a kigatsuku girl do now?" Then I'd
run and get the dustpan. I recognized my mother's teaching when
I read that wonderful scripture: "Verily, I say, [you] should be
anxiously engaged in a good cause, and do many things
of [your] own free will, and bring to pass much righteousness;
For the power is in [you], wherein [you] are [an agent]
unto [yourself]." (D&C 58:27–28.)*
—CHIEKO N. OKAZAKI ("SPIT AND MUD," 1992)

The first time I heard of *kigatsuku* (key-got-sue-koo), I was
sitting in a leadership meeting. Our director talked to us about
what it means to be a leader. He mentioned the word *kigatsuku*
and tried to explain what it meant. He told us it was a way
of being. I remember thinking the closest word in English is
initiative. The rest of that meeting is a blur, but learning about
kigatsuku changed my life.

My father served a mission in Japan, so I asked him to
explain to me the word and its meaning. He wrote: *"Kigatsuku*

37

means (1) notice; become aware (conscious) of; be attentive. (2) come to oneself; recover consciousness. The *kanjis,* or parts of the words, break down as follows: *Ki* is the same as *genki,* which means 'spirit' or 'feelings.' *Tsuku* is the verb for 'to stick to,' 'to catch fire,' or 'to be lighted.' So, it's basically saying, 'My spirit or feelings are energized.'"

Since learning about kigatsuku, I have sought to have my spirit energized and act without being told. It is also a trait I look for in others, and I try to surround myself with those who have it.

A kigatsuku person is the first to do the dishes when the meal is over, the first to take out the trash when it is full, the first to include everyone, and the first to notice a need before it is pointed out. Those who have kigatsuku are not compelled. No one has to ask them to help out or coax them into awareness. They sit with the person who is alone, they are quick to say thank you, and they are often close to the Spirit. Kigatsuku people take initiative, are anxiously engaged, and don't bring attention to themselves. They serve because it is in their nature to do so. They uplift because they don't know any other way. They are energized with faith and hope, and the energy they emit is contagious. Can you think of anyone in your life who has kigatsuku? People who embody kigatsuku stand apart. You notice them because they inspire you to be better and to pay more attention. In his book *Leadership,* Elder Sterling W. Sill said:

> *There are a great many stowaways in the Church who hide out in spiritual idleness, hoping to make the journey*

without either working or paying their way. Woe to him
who has lost his initiative. Woe to him who develops
battle fatigue. Woe to him who does nothing. The law
says, "Get thee up and be illuminated." The alternative
is to stay down and be eliminated. (1958, 110)

Here are two of my favorite stories that exemplify kigatsuku.

The Milk-Crate Hoop

Years ago while visiting my family in Northern California,
I was riding in the car with my dad and little brother. Suddenly,
my dad asked us if it was okay if he pulled over for a few
minutes to talk with some kids. Since we weren't in a hurry
we said yes, and after driving a short distance my dad stopped
in front of a makeshift basketball court. He got out and started
taking a few things out of the back of his truck. I saw a basketball
hoop and some tools. It didn't take me long to figure out my
father's plans. The kids playing on the basketball court had
knocked out the bottom of an empty milk crate and nailed it to
the backboard as a makeshift basketball hoop. I guess at some
point Dad had seen this and wanted to get them a real basketball
hoop. I sat there in awe as my father took the basketball hoop
he had bought and used his tools to put it up for the boys. They
seemed shocked and didn't say much, but they were obviously
happy.

Once my father finished his little project, he collected his
tools, got in the truck, and we left. We didn't talk about what he
had just done—it was simply part of who he is. I sat in silence
the rest of the way home and had to fight back tears.

The Prom Dress

I was one of those lucky girls who had the opportunity to attend prom with a great guy. Prom was a blast, but I'll be honest—as much fun as I had with my date and our friends, none of that could compare with what happened before the night even started.

My mom is an amazing seamstress, so she and I had picked out a dress pattern and found the perfect material. At that time, I was one of seven kids, which kept my mom busy, so the making of my prom dress (like most dresses made by Mom) happened in the wee hours of the night and right up to the night before prom. Mom and I had decided on a beautiful green satin. The dress pattern was simple. It was an empire waist with a bow that tied in the back. We decided we would turn the material inside out for the top of the dress and leave the satin side for the bottom of the dress. The pattern wasn't very formal-looking, but the satin material made it more elegant. Mom went to task making the dress. She had me stand for measurements, and all was well—or so I thought.

The night before prom, Mom brought the dress to me for final touch-ups, and I all but gasped. I tried really hard for a girl of sixteen not to cry, but the dress looked horrible. I knew my mom had been slaving away to make this dress for me, so I certainly didn't want to seem ungrateful, but the dress hadn't turned out like we intended. Mom could see it too, and she apologized, but since it was the night before prom, there wasn't much either of us could do. I sucked it up and resigned myself to just wearing the dress to prom. The idea Mom and I had for the dress was a good one, but the material ended up looking too simple on top, so it just looked awful. I also felt terrible because I knew I wasn't doing a good job of hiding the fact that I didn't like the dress, but I was trying so hard for my mom's sake. I went to bed, crushed that my prom dream wasn't going to come true. I had the dream date but not the dream dress I had imagined.

When I woke up in the morning, the first thing I thought of was how determined I was to make myself get into that dress and smile and greet my date that night. I knew I had to be strong, because the last thing I wanted to do was to hurt my mom's feelings. Those thoughts quickly evaporated when I saw my dress hanging on my bedroom door. This was not the same dress I had tried on the night before. My mom had stayed up the entire night and unpicked the entire bodice of my dress by hand. She had gone out and bought some white satin material and had completely redone my dress. I couldn't believe it! My mom had sensed my disappointment and decided to fix the dress even if it meant she wouldn't sleep that night. She had seven other kids to take care of early the next morning, so I knew what a sacrifice it had been for her. But my mother saw a need and filled it unselfishly.

Kigatsuku is hard to describe, but you will recognize it in people if you are looking. If it isn't something that comes natural to you, you can certainly work on practicing and applying it more in your life. Be the one to sit next to someone who is alone at church. Be the one to say something positive about someone that others are tearing down. Eat lunch with the coworker everyone else dislikes and gossips about. Go get your visiting or home teaching done early in the month and follow

41

up on any commitments you have them make, or that you have made to them. Listen to what someone you care about needs, and fill that need. Instead of feeling lonely on the weekend, open up your home as a place for people to get together. The more you develop kigatsuku in your own life, the more you will be attracted to other people that have it. This characteristic is not only addictive, it's also very contagious.

Action Questions

- Do you have kigatsuku? What is one thing you can focus on to have more?
- In what areas would you like to take more initiative? What attainable goals can you set?
- How can you cultivate a less self-focused outlook?
- How can you better listen to and recognize the needs of others, and then help fill those needs?

FOUR
Make It Happen

If you can dream it—you can do it!
—WALT DISNEY

What do you dream about at night when no one else is around and all you can hear is your heart? What place, thing, or achievement do your thoughts wander to when they aren't focused on anything else? What do you wish you had but don't?

When I asked numerous people about their dreams, they got excited and said things like, "I want to go to Africa," or "I want to learn how to play the piano," or they would tell me they wanted to learn how to sew, write, paint, play the guitar, etc. But when I asked them how they planned to accomplish their dreams, most of them didn't really have a plan.

It is natural to dream about things, to long for exotic places, to wish you had more talents, and so on. What is not natural or easy is making your dreams become reality. A favorite book of mine, Sterling W. Still's *Leadership,* is filled with amazing principles about making things happen in our lives. Elder Sill said this about the process of turning ideas into action:

Many ideas die en route. They never live through the process or ordeal of being translated into action. Yet it is this ability to get ideas successfully through the early stages of their metamorphosis to where they become faith and action that has real value. (113)

I think we have all had many ideas we never translated into action. The excuse may be money, lack of time, fear of failure, or simply being unfamiliar with the process.

In this chapter, we will focus on principles that will help you to make things happen in your life. We will talk about how to set goals and accomplish them. We will discuss what it takes to make your dreams come true. And we will talk about how others can help us along the way.

To illustrate these principles, I will share a little of my journey. My college major was English literature with a minor in linguistics. I also took a few editing classes, figuring they might help me in my personal writing. When I graduated, those editing classes helped me land a job as a copyeditor for a local magazine. I liked the job but realized quickly the life of an editor wasn't for me. I needed to work with people.

During that time I was teaching released-time seminary, and I loved it. Unfortunately, I did not get hired to teach full-time. I was devastated. Being a seminary teacher felt so right to me, and nothing else seemed to make as much sense. I felt a deep sense of loss. I'd been heading in a certain direction, and now I had abruptly come to a stop. I got a job at a residential treatment center for troubled teen girls, but I didn't have a clue what I wanted to do with my life. In addition to all of that, I wasn't dating at all.

For months, I was depressed and drained. None of my plans and dreams were coming to fruition. I decided that because I had a college degree and didn't really know what to do, I had failed. I enlisted the help of many friends, family members, coworkers—pretty much anyone who knew me—thinking they might help me figure out my next step in life. Of course, everyone I spoke with gave me advice. Some suggested I go to grad school, while others said I should find any job I liked. I made a list of things I liked, passions I had, things I was good at, etc. I spent many nights pleading with the Lord to help me find my place, and many lonely hours struggling to discover what I wanted to do or what I was *supposed* to do with my life.

I was surprised when my answer finally came. While visiting my family in California for Christmas, I was in the front room one day, talking with my mom and sister. I was complaining about how, despite all my prayers and efforts, I still couldn't figure out what to do with my life. I said I was starting to feel paralyzed. My mom and sister started to bounce ideas around, and my sister said I should definitely work with people. She said I seemed to have a great ability to work with teens and their parents—especially in difficult situations, from which many other people shy away. She didn't say the words *social work,* but I clearly heard them in my mind as she was speaking. Something just clicked into place for me in that moment. My sister's simple words sparked the first of many big changes in my life. Figuring out what to do with my life proved to be much more difficult than actually making it happen.

After talking to my sister, I immediately started looking for a job in the field of social work, and almost on a whim joined AmeriCorps' Volunteer in Service to America (VISTA) program. I would describe it as sort of a domestic Peace Corps. I took a job as the volunteer and recruitment coordinator at a small nonprofit company in downtown Boston. Moving across the country, working in a big city, working with mentors and teens—all these things made sense to me.

Once in Boston I was able to look back on what brought me there and see the hand of the Lord all along the way. Getting off the T, the Boston public subway, walking to my building downtown, climbing the stairs, and arriving at my office for my new job was empowering. I had a feeling of being free.

I remember watching one of the X-Men movies and there was a scene that described exactly how I felt. One of the mutant characters, Angel, grew wings out of his back. His father wanted him to be normal—to get rid of his wings. So he sat in this chair, strapped in, waiting to be given a shot that would change him. When the time came for him to receive the shot, Angel couldn't do it. He burst out of the chair and flew out the window. He was free. When I saw that scene for the first time, I felt such a great sense of relief. I had been stifled and trapped, and once I made some decisions with the guidance of the Spirit, I was free, and I became almost addicted to making things happen in my life. Thus, my motto, Make It Happen, was born.

The Make It Happen concept is nothing new. It simply is what it implies. It's making things happen in your life, not hoping things will happen or waiting for others to make things happen in your life. It's figuring out what you want and going after it. Of course it's important to be in tune with the Spirit. Go to the Lord with your plans, desires, goals, and dreams. Let

Him be a part of making things happen in your life. He can do so much more for you than you could ever do for yourself.

The process of making things happen in your life is not always easy. If it were, everyone we associate with would be in a state of happiness, living out his or her dreams. There is cost involved in making things happen, and you have to be willing to pay the price.

PAYING THE PRICE

I have been blessed with many amazing friends who have taught me valuable, life-long lessons. Through their examples, I have realized the necessity of being willing to pay the price. The lessons I've learned from the following three examples helped me discover that I had the power to make things happen in my life.

Experience One: Education versus Travel

When I was twenty years old, I traveled to Jerusalem and Egypt with a BYU study-abroad program. I was beyond excited as this would be my first "real" travel experience. I have seven siblings, so traveling has always been difficult and expensive for my family. Therefore, going to Jerusalem and Egypt was a dream come true for me. While overlooking Old Jerusalem one day, I struck up a conversation with a fellow student in my program. He started to tell me about all of his travel experiences. I was flabbergasted by all the places he had been and the things he had seen and done at such a young age. In fact, I was completely and entirely envious and angry at him for it. How could he afford such luxuries?

47

A few days later, he and I were walking around the Jerusalem Center and ended up sitting by a small grove of olive trees. I will never forget that short but life-changing conversation. This fellow student asked me why I hadn't traveled more, since he could tell from our conversations that I value traveling. His question made me a bit angry at first, and I quickly reacted by letting him know that unlike him, I couldn't afford to travel. He laughed at my reply and very gently shared why that was just an excuse. He asked me if I had a job back home. I said yes. He asked me what I spend my money on. I said I spent it on college. Then he paused. He went on to tell me that he too had a job back home, but instead of spending his money on education he spent it all on traveling, since that was what he valued most at the time. He said that if I was willing to take all the money I spent on my education and instead spent it on travel, I could have the same kinds of experiences he was having.

It was so simple, yet the very idea had never crossed my mind. I was making a choice. Despite my great desire to travel, I placed a higher value on getting my education, since that was where I was spending my money. I was in control, and if I wanted to I could've traveled instead of going to school. Although I hadn't really thought of it before, I wasn't willing to pay the price of sacrificing or postponing my education. That simple conversation was a huge epiphany for me.

Experience Two: Natural versus Acquired Skill

A few years after my study-abroad experience, I went to Idaho to be an Especially for Youth (EFY) counselor. The coordinator—my supervisor—quickly became a mentor for whom I had great respect and admiration. I was particularly in awe of his seemingly endless amount of spiritual knowledge. He seemed to have every scripture memorized. He always had a quote from an apostle on the tip of his tongue. Again, I was completely envious. It hardly seemed fair that someone that young could be so well versed in the gospel.

One night as I was quietly studying my scriptures in the lobby, my mentor came over and sat next to me. Without ever really intending to do so, we began a great journey in the scriptures, and I was truly enlightened on many levels. I couldn't believe the insight he had. We connected scripture chains that provided me with greater understanding of gospel principles. I marveled over what I had learned in our short study, but I was also still extremely envious of his ability. After I thanked him for spending time with me and sharing his insights, I knew he could sense I was frustrated. I asked him how he could do it—how in the short time we had just spent together studying, he had helped me to learn more than I had learned during my own personal scripture study that entire year. He simply said, "I paid the price."

I was a little shocked by his answer, because I had assumed he was just really spiritual or naturally gifted when it came to the scriptures. He explained that although he and I had only studied the scriptures together for a short time, he had shown me things he had learned during years of study. He talked about the hours he had spent cross-referencing the scriptures and digging into the meaning of things so he could better understand the principles the scriptures teach. He said, and this has changed my life, that for some things there's just no shortcut—you have to pay the price.

In both of the above experiences, I felt envious and made assumptions. In both cases I was wrong. Both of these friends taught me great lessons about the importance of paying the price in time, study, and due diligence. Gratefully, the Lord allowed me to share this same lesson a few years later.

Experience Three: The Price of Playing the Piano

A friend of mine asked me to play the piano for her to sing in church. Accompanying a vocal number wasn't anything out of the ordinary, so we practiced, Sunday came, and we did our musical number in sacrament meeting. After the meeting, a girl came up to me and complimented me on my piano-playing ability. She said something to the effect that it came so easy to me and she wished she could play like that. Many times when people sing or play the piano, people compliment them, but for some reason that day, instead of just saying thank you, I told her my story.

When my mom was a little girl, she wanted to play the piano, but when things got tough she asked her mom if she could quit, and her mom let her. So my mother never really learned to play the piano. As a result—I'm sure many of you can relate to this—she decided all her children were going to take piano lessons and she wouldn't allow them to quit. For me this meant that when I turned seven I started piano lessons, and I continued to take lessons until I graduated from high school. Taking piano lessons was non-negotiable—believe me, I tried for years to get out of them! So I continued to play, had a few different teachers, and got plenty of opportunities in the Church to share my talents. By the time the girl in my ward was telling me it looked so easy for me to play the piano, I'd been playing for about twenty years. In my mind I was thinking, "I hope I sound good and it looks easy, because I've been playing my entire life." I think I told her something to that effect and that she could play the piano but she would have to work on it for a long time—it isn't a skill that comes easily.

These experiences, along with many others, play a huge part in my life when it comes to making things happen. There really are no shortcuts to success! I have learned and continue to learn that you can have what you want but you have to be willing to pay the price—sometimes literally.

SETTING GOALS

In order to make things happen in your life, you have to have goals, dreams, and expectations—and write them down. The simple act of writing these things down seems to transform them from wishes or dreams in your heart into goals that can be accomplished and become reality. I know there are a gazillion and one books out there that teach, much better than I can, the art of setting goals. There are books about how to set goals, long-term goals, five-year plans, short-term goals, and so much more. I want to share a way I have discovered to set life-long goals. If you use this method, you will be able to set goals and make things happen in your life.

One day on my mission in San Diego, my companion and I met a visitor to our ward. She was a member of the Church from somewhere in the Midwest, nowhere near the ocean. I will never forget this girl because she changed the way I thought about goal setting. As we were talking to her and asking the usual questions, she said she was in San Diego to learn how to surf. I thought that was cool so I asked her how long she would be in town. She went on to tell us that she was taking a surfing class that lasted six weeks and then she would go back home. I was curious what had brought her to San Diego, since she didn't know anyone there. (She later explained that she was staying in hostels.) She told my companion and me that on the last day of her mission, before she went to bed in the mission home, she wrote down 101 goals she wanted to accomplish in her life. One of the goals on her list was to learn how to surf. It had been about six years since she had returned from her mission, and the time had come to make it happen.

I was impressed and motivated. I even wrote my own list of 101 goals (which is a lot harder than you think) in the mission home on the last day of my mission. Here's where I changed it up a bit. My 101 goals were anything in life from getting married and reading stories to my children, to singing with a full orchestra and owning a piano. They were all over the place. Some I had control over and some I didn't. From my list, I chose five goals I had complete control over (you can choose any number, but I'd stay between three and ten). This didn't mean it would be easy to accomplish the five goals; it just meant I had the ability, knew where to gain the ability, or knew someone with the ability to help me accomplish the goals. Like short-term goals, they were each measurable and specific, but unlike short-term goals, there was no date by which they had to be accomplished. And they weren't in any particular order. Here are my five On the Way goals:

- Sit on the steps at the Piazza de Spagna ("Spanish Steps") in Rome, Italy.

- Own a piano.
- Write a book.
- Sing a solo live with an orchestra.
- Record a CD of original songs.

On the Way

Jesus Christ performed many of His miracles while He was on the way to somewhere else. You will recall the story of Jairus and how he pled with Christ to save his twelve-year-old daughter, who was deathly ill. While Christ was on his way to heal the girl, a woman with an issue of blood that had lasted for twelve years came behind Him and touched His hem. Her faith was simple: If she could touch Him, she would be healed. (See Luke 8:41–56.)

There are many more New Testament stories where miracles happened, people were healed, and lives were changed when the Lord was on His way to do something else. I believe in this principle and have had great success with it in my life. That is why there is no completion date for my five On the Way goals. I plan to accomplish them on the way to achieving other goals and dreams in my life. These types of goals usually fall into two categories: (1) Goals that happen because you make them happen on your own, and (2) Goals that happen with the help of others because you put your goals out there.

On My Own

It is important to set goals or have dreams in your life that you have control over. There are many things, such as marriage, that you don't have as much control over. Making a goal you have control over means you already have everything you need to make the goal happen, even if it will be difficult or expensive. You may need to work a little more, find time off, or do some research to make your dreams come true, but you can do it on your own. Two of my On the Way goals were accomplished on my own.

Italy

I had wanted to go to Italy for years. I even took some private lessons in the Italian language so I would be able to communicate when I traveled there. The problem was I always seemed to have an excuse for not going. Either I couldn't find anyone to go with me, or it was too expensive. One day I was talking to my mom and she asked me why I hadn't gone to Italy yet. I gave her one of my excuses and went on my way, but for whatever reason her question stayed with me all day. So, after years of talking about it and trying to get people to come with me to Italy, I finally decided to stop waiting for others, or using money as an excuse, and I went to Italy on my own. I was able to visit Venice, Rome, and Florence, as well as some other beautiful places along the way. I sat on the Spanish Steps and reveled in the satisfaction of making my dream come true.

Writing a Book

I have wanted to write a book for as long as I can remember. In talking with people over the years, I learned that *most* people want to write a book. They are full of exciting ideas they want to share. I love hearing about people's ideas and often ask, "If you could write a book, what would be about?" In answering my own question one day, I realized I wanted to write a book about things I've learned being single and how they've helped me. And so I began my journey. It has been years of writing, lots of editing, many people reading and sharing ideas, and a labor of love to finish this book. I am so happy I had this goal and was able to make it happen.

Putting It Out There

While it is empowering to make things happen in your life, sometimes you need help to do so. Sometimes you need to rely on others.

I believe in taking your goals, dreams, and desires and putting them out there in the universe. Letting people know what you want in life helps them to be a part of your Make It Happen process. We often accomplish great things with the help of others. I would not have been able to accomplish two of my On the Way goals without the help of others.

Recording a CD of Original Songs

I have always loved music, and I started composing songs when I was about fourteen years old. Years later, after writing enough songs to fill an album, I wanted to make a CD of original songs to give to my family and friends for Christmas. The problem was I didn't have the money to pay for time at a recording studio, I didn't have any connections, and I didn't even know how to begin the process.

At FHE one day, I mentioned wanting to find a studio or work with someone, and a guy in my ward overheard me. He told me he had a recording studio and wanted to try out some of his new equipment, and that he would be willing to work with me for free. I couldn't believe it! We began the recording process, and I learned so much. In the end I had a CD of nine original songs. I was able to give the CD to my parents for Christmas just before I left on my mission.

Adopting a Piano

I told my roommates how much I wanted to have a piano in our home, and we started talking about renting one. My best friend heard me talking about wanting a piano and told me that his grandmother had recently died. He wondered if I wanted her baby grand piano. I was ecstatic! I adopted that Wurlitzer, named her Ellie May (after her previous owner), and even had an open house when we got her into our home. I had wanted my own piano my whole life, and I finally had one.

MISSION (ALMOST) ACCOMPLISHED

Whether you make your dreams and goals come true on your own or with a little help from other people, making things happen in your life can be empowering and addicting. I still want to sing a live solo with an orchestra one day, and look I forward to making that happen.

Now that I've shared with you how I accomplished most of my On the Way goals, I hope you realize you really can make things happen in your life. When you are living intentionally, acting rather than being acted upon, things happen in your life that help you accomplish your goals.

As you write down your goals and strive to make them happen, the Lord gives you tender mercies along the way. These may come through people who help you reach your goals, through jobs where you earn the money to reach your goals, or through inspiration as to how you can reach your goals. You may not be expecting to accomplish a certain goal any time soon, and the next thing you know you can check it off your list. It is the act of setting a goal, striving to make it happen, living intentionally, and learning to live the On the Way principle that will help you move forward in your life. It is a glorious feeling to set goals in your life and check them off. I hope you feel empowered in your life to do so. Stop making excuses and putting things off. Make it happen!

Action Questions

- What are your dreams? What is holding you back from accomplishing those dreams that are within your control?
- What is one thing you want to change about your life within the next six months? Be sure to choose something you have absolute control over.
- How can the Lord help you fulfill your dreams?
- What price do you need to pay to accomplish your dreams? What do you need to do to pay that price?
- Is there a skill or attribute you want to acquire? What goals can you set to help you acquire it?
- Come up with 101 goals you want to accomplish in your life.
- How can you seek the help of others in reaching your goals?
- How can you help someone else accomplish one of his or her goals?

FIVE

Purple Hair

If a man loses pace with his companions, perhaps it is because he hears a different drummer. Let him step to the music which he hears, however measured, or far away.
—HENRY DAVID THOREAU

The worst thing you can do as a single person is to become stagnant in life. To get stuck in a rut, to become mediocre, or to just accept the status quo can make you miserable. And yet it is so easy to do. You get comfortable with where you are, and you settle in for the long haul. This is the fastest way I know to become unhappy.

I grew up in a home that was loud, busy, and anything but ordinary. Variety was the name of the game. My mom would sing in the kitchen, my dad would sometimes bring home flowers he bought from some guy on the side of the road, and with eight children in the family it was rarely, if ever, quiet. When my mom embarrassed us kids, we would ask her to stop and just be normal. I've never forgotten what she would say: "You don't want an ordinary mom like everyone else, do you?" She was right—I loved how my mom mixed things up. Because of the fun-loving environment my parents fostered in our home, my siblings and I had friends over all the time. My dad would make malts, my mom cooked a ton of food, and we stocked our freezer with all kinds of ice cream.

VARIETY IS THE SPICE OF LIFE

Everyone needs variety in his or her life. Some people, like me, need *a lot* of variety, while some people just need a little. Make sure you're getting the variety you need in your life. Variety or change doesn't have to involve big things like moving out of state, getting a new job, or even being more social. Sometimes variety comes in little unexpected ways on ordinary days. Below are three experiences I've had where variety, fun, and changing things up a little made a difference in my life.

The Mary Poppins Drawer

One day a few years ago, when I was working at a nonprofit in downtown Boston, I was talking to my coworker and she stopped midsentence. She looked up at me and asked, "Why do you think they put baby carrots in salad?" I laughed out loud. She went on, "It's not like you can comfortably stab the carrot with your fork, and it's just not kosher to go picking through your salad. So what are they thinking?"

After a good laugh I went about my day, and my coworker went about hers. At one point I noticed her rummaging through her drawer for something. First, let me tell you a little about this drawer. It has everything inside, and when I say everything, I pretty much mean it. Every day she'd take something new out of it or put something random into it. The drawer seemed to spontaneously toss out gum, twenty-four hours a day. So there

I was laughing out loud at her. She looked over at me very seriously, because she was actually working—we did that sometimes. I couldn't help it—I had the perfect name for her drawer of tricks: the Mary Poppins drawer. You know the bag Mary Poppins has in the movie, the one the lamp, rug, etc., come out of? Yeah, that was my coworker's drawer. Well, the nickname stuck, and soon the rest of our coworkers knew about the Mary Poppins drawer, mostly because they needed something from it at some point.

Jelly Beans

In that same office around Easter time, my coworker thought it would be funny to pull random candy from the Mary Poppins Drawer throughout the day, to guess which was my favorite. Since I'm not a huge candy/sweets fan, this went on for days. She would pull a new candy out of the drawer, I would shake my head no, and she would decide what to choose next. We laughed a lot, but my coworker started to get a bit frustrated that she couldn't figure out my favorite candy.

And then it happened. One day, she pulled out a bag of jelly beans and she could tell by my reaction that she had figured it out. I can't help it—I'm a sucker for jelly beans. I just love the little things. It doesn't matter what brand, if they are speckled or not, or even what colors they are, I just love them. So my coworker bought all kinds of jelly beans and stashed them in all the different drawers and cubbies of my desk. Soon my other coworkers took notice and would end up taking "jelly-bean breaks." Then our volunteers caught wind of the jelly-bean stash, and it even spread to the nonprofit next door.

I was amazed at how those little candies could bring people together. For the rest of the year I worked in that office, I would find a bag of jelly beans randomly placed in my desk drawer just when I was about to run out. People would eat the jelly beans out of my drawer, and then people would replenish it. And now whenever I see or eat jelly beans, I can't help but remember those good days.

Purple Hair

The last experience happened this past Christmas. I was home in California with my family when I got an envelope in the mail from one of my good friends. I was instructed to wait until Christmas to open the envelope, so I did. When the day came, I opened the envelope to find a purple hair extension. I was elated! A few weeks before, while with this friend, I'd seen a girl with bright purple hair walk by. I told my friend that deep down inside I wanted to dye my hair purple. She looked at me, laughed, and said, "Don't do it." So instead she gave me a little lock of purple hair for Christmas. Every once in a while, to this day, I clip the purple lock of hair into my hair. I absolutely love the reactions it brings.

Laughing at life, bringing people together through food, creating spontaneous love moments, and a streak of purple hair are just a few of the ways I maintain variety in my life. Some other mix-it-up things I have done are traveling, becoming a mentor, tackling new challenges, and learning new skills.

LEARN SOMETHING NEW

Most people are content to just stick with what they know. A friend of mine once said he didn't want to try new things because he didn't know if he would be good at them—and he *has* to be good at everything he does. While I can see his point, I think he is missing out on a lot of opportunities to meet new people and gain new skills. Who knows, he may actually be good at something he's never done before. In addition to adding variety to your life, learning new things can help you to develop skills and meet new people. Learning new things isn't always easy, but it usually pays off.

Once my roommate and I turned an old TV into a terrarium for our pet turtle. It was a major project but so much fun. We even got the knob that used to turn the TV on and off connected to a switch that turned the terrarium light on and off. That same roommate and I got some friends together and made some really funny videos.

I have taken language lessons a few times from friends and enjoyed it very much. As I mentioned previously, before I went to Italy, I took Italian from a friend who had served his mission there. And during my commute for grad school and my internships, I began learning Japanese in my car. There are so many adventures to be had, so many skills to learn, and so much to discover.

Here are some ways to add variety to your life:
- Take a new route to class or work.
- Look for restaurants and shops you've never been to and go inside.
- Listen to a type of music you usually don't listen to.
- Learn a new skill or pick up a hobby.
- Try new foods.

- Travel.
- Explore the city or state you live in. Buy a travel guide or ask people about their favorite places.
- Meet new friends and different type of people.
- Hold a music night and invite people who sing or play a musical instrument.
- Set up a big group activity like bowling, a YouTube favorites night, or visiting a water park.
- Teach a skill to others.
- Give gifts to your friends or family members for no reason at all.

If you find yourself getting stuck or feeling like you are in a rut, simply add some variety to your life. It is amazing how a little change in your course can make such a big difference in your destination.

Action Questions

- What can you do to create variety in your current schedule?
- What changes do you need to make, like attending graduate school, getting a new job, or moving into a new house or new ward?
- How can you invite new opportunities into your life?
- What can you do to bring variety to others' lives?

SIX
A Matter of Heart

The Sassover Rebbe said that he learned the meaning of love from overhearing a conversation between two villagers. One asked the other, "Do you love me?" The second replied, "I love you deeply." The first asked, "Do you know, my friend, what gives me pain?" The second protested that he could not possibly know. "If you do not know what gives me pain," lamented the first, "how can you say you love me?"
—RABBI DAVID WOLPE *(MAKING LOSS MATTER,* 1999)

I love reading, studying, and teaching about hearts. Often, the word *heart* and the word *love* are used interchangeably. We know the heart muscle is the focal point in our body and keeps us alive physically. We also know that love, the focal point of our souls, keeps us alive spiritually. The idea of love and hearts has been written about for centuries. They are the debated topics of scholars and the conversations of common people. Have you ever pondered the question, Is it better to love or be loved? Poet and writer Robert A. Johnson said this about love:

We can learn that human relationship is inseparable from friendship and commitment. We can learn the essence of love is not to use the other person to make us happy but to serve and affirm the one we love. And we can discover, to our surprise, that what we have needed more than anything was not so much to be loved, as to love. (Johnson, *Romantic Love,* 1983, 201)

I have my days when I just want to be loved, but most days I find great satisfaction giving love. One of my favorite poets, Rainer Maria Rilke, said: "To love is good, too: love being difficult. For one human being to love another: that is perhaps the most difficult of all our tasks, the ultimate, the last test and proof, the work for which all other work is preparation" (Rilke, *Letters,* 1934, 54).

I agree with Rilke that love is difficult and tests us in ways we can't imagine. At the same time, I know love can be almost effortless and can come when we least expect it.

THE VALUE OF HEARTS

In the Church, there is a lot of talk about taking care of our bodies, protecting them, not violating them, and being chaste. We talk about what we should and shouldn't put on our bodies and in our bodies. We talk about how our bodies are not our own and how they are "bought with a price." We even talk about how our bodies are in the image of our Heavenly Father. But what about our hearts? We learn how we are responsible for our own bodies and for what we do to other people's bodies. We learn how sacred our bodies are and the role they play in the plan of happiness. We discuss how our choices—what we see, what we hear, what we say, and what we do—involve our bodies. With all this emphasis on our bodies, I'm fully convinced that the Lord also values our hearts.

In my opinion, we will be responsible for what we allow others to do with our hearts and how we treat theirs. I think we are accountable for the hearts we mislead, the hearts we break, the hearts we make commitments to, and the hearts we love. Likewise, we will be held accountable for letting others break our hearts and for giving our heart to others. The prophet Brigham Young declared, "Let our anxiety be centered upon one thing, the sanctification of our own hearts, the purifying of our own affections" (Young, *Discourses of Brigham Young,* 1925, 180). The Lord told Samuel, "The Lord seeth not as man seeth; for man looketh on the outward appearance, but the Lord looketh on the heart" (1 Samuel 16:7). If the Lord is concerned with hearts—and He truly is—we should be as well.

THE STUDY OF HEARTS

While serving a mission, I learned the importance of communication. Sometimes words were necessary, but most of the time it was all about the communication of the heart or the Spirit. About seven months into my mission, I was called to serve in American Sign Language (ASL). Although I knew colloquial sign, I didn't know the missionary discussions or religious signs, and I was very rusty in the ASL I did know. It didn't take long to realize that my inability to sign well was hindering my communication. I was struggling to learn the discussions in ASL, feeling isolated as the only ASL missionary in my mission at the time, and wondering how I could teach the Deaf.

My mission president suggested that if we were struggling in a certain area of our lives or with certain investigators on specific topics, we should study that topic or subject in the scriptures. I don't think I had ever studied the Book of Mormon by topic before, so it was a new concept to me. I began looking over the scriptures, wondering what topic to study. Since I had been thinking a lot about communication, I started to skim over my scriptures, looking for the passages about how the Lord communicates with others.

Soon, a pattern emerged that I hadn't noticed before. Whenever the Lord was communicating to others, there seemed to be something surrounding that dialogue about the Spirit or about the people's hearts. When I got to Alma 9, I realized there was a heart pattern. In that chapter, I put a small sticky note that reads, "How many times is the word *heart* mentioned in the Book of Mormon?" After writing that question, I started reading the Book of Mormon again, underlining the word *heart* every time I saw it. Recently, by typing my question into Google, I learned that the word *heart* is used in the Book of Mormon 431 times! Obviously, the Lord cares about our hearts. An amazing change came upon me when I read the Book of Mormon through a heart lens.

"AFTER MINE OWN HEART"

In the Book of Mormon I marked up during my "heart journey" on my mission, I wrote a few questions in the margins. One of the questions is "Who is holding my heart?" Later I wrote, "Do I give Satan power over my heart?" In other words, who is holding my heart, guiding my life? Is it God, or is it

Satan? At some point I took the quote "Who is holding my heart?" and tacked it on my cork board to remind me of the choices I make each day about my heart. Another question I wrote in my scriptures is "What treasure is my heart set upon?" I also wrote the question "How hard is my heart?"

The scriptures are replete with examples of men and women who turned their hearts to God and were blessed. There are also many scriptural examples of those who turned their hearts against God and received condemnation. Wars were won and lost based on who had their hearts set upon God and who did not. Kingdoms were built and destroyed contingent upon who yielded their hearts to the Lord. Kings rose in glory with God's help, and fell in infamy when they turned their hearts away.

One such king stands out in my mind: David. In his youth, he set his heart upon God and His righteousness. David killed the Philistine giant, Goliath, but he became so much more than that miraculous event. The Lord said concerning David, "The Lord hath sought him a man after his own heart" (1 Samuel 13:14). God knew David had the heart of a king. In the New Testament the Lord declared, "I have found David, a man after mine own heart, which shall fulfill all my will" (Acts 13:22). God knew David's heart. He loved David and was ready to give him every possible blessing.

This reminds me of another man after the Lord's heart. In Helaman 10:5, the Lord tells Nephi, "All things shall be done unto thee according to thy word, for thou shalt not ask that which is contrary to my will." God knew Nephi's heart. He knew Nephi had His will written upon his heart. Both King David and Nephi understood that if their hearts belonged to

God, they could do no wrong. Tragically, David closed off his heart to God and, in doing so, lost everything. My heart aches for David when I read of his life. He had everything and lost it because of his carnal desires. If King David, beloved of God and a "man after [His] own heart," can be led astray, how do *I* become someone who is after the manner of God's heart?

It takes continuous faith and action to yield one's heart to God. In Helaman 3:35 we read:

> *Nevertheless they did fast and pray oft, and did wax stronger and stronger in their humility, and firmer and firmer in the faith of Christ, unto the filling their souls with joy and consolation, yea, even to the purifying and the sanctification of their hearts, which sanctification cometh because of their yielding their hearts unto God.*

The only way to know and do God's will is to yield my heart to His. In doing so, I learn of Him and become more like Him. So the big question is, What consumes your heart? If I were to ask your closest friends or family to describe you, where would they tell me your heart lies? Is your heart after the manner of God? Do you seek His will, or are you after the manner of men or yourself? I love how C.S. Lewis describes how God must feel about us.

> *Christ says, Give me All. I don't want so much of your time and so much of your money and so much of your work: I want You. I have not come to torment your*

natural self, but to kill it. No half-measures are any good. I don't want to cut off a branch here and a branch there, I want to have the whole tree down. I don't want to drill the tooth, or crown it, or stop it, but to have it out. Hand over the whole natural self, all the desires which you think innocent as well as the ones you think wicked—the whole outfit. I will give you a new self instead. In fact, I will give you Myself: My own will shall become yours. (Lewis, *Mere Christianity*, 1952, 153)

I want to be that kind of a person. I want to give my will to God. I want to be like Nephi, and like King David before his fall. I want to be a woman after the manner of God's heart, but I find myself, like David, following after the lusts of man. The selfish part of my heart, the part that is impatient and unyielding, wants blessings and promises fulfilled *now*—not on God's time or in His manner. Because of the worldly parts of my heart, I am grateful to a God who allows me to go through trials, tests my faith, and allows me to feel after Him. While I can't say I am grateful for some of the trials in my life, I am indebted to the Lord for the lessons I have learned from them. I believe the Lord allows us to go through certain experiences so that our hearts will seek after Him. One such incident in my life completely changed my heart.

GRANT'S GIFT

By the time I had been single and on my own for an entire year—yes, that made me a whoppin' nineteen years old—I thought I had love all figured out. My heart ached for family members and friends who had died. My heart rejoiced for people who had fallen in love and gotten married. I had seen and felt a lot of love in my short nineteen years, but I had no idea what was about to happen in my life and to my heart.

On July 24, 1999, my fifteen-year-old brother died. I remember talking with Grant in the morning before he went out to play with his best friend, and late that night I was waiting for his body to be found in a nearby canal. My heart had never felt so much pain! I didn't know anyone could survive such agony. For a long time, I felt crippled by sorrow and anguish.

During this time of darkness, there was some light in the form of the gospel, my amazing family, and hearts that were listening. I learned so many lessons from this experience, but I like to call the one that entirely changed my life "Grant's Gift." My brother's life and death completely changed not only my life but also the way I think about hearts. His sudden and unexpected death was a wake-up call for me. I realized how delicate and short life can be. I struggled with not being able to say goodbye to Grant and wondered if he knew how much I really loved him.

Then I started to think about my life. I wondered if each person in my life knew how I felt about him or her. Questions started filling my mind, questions like, If I were to die tomorrow, would people know what they mean to me? From that moment on I have strived to let the people in my life know how much I love and appreciate them. As my heart communicates with other hearts, I am empowered and all my relationships are strengthened.

THE SOUND OF HEARTS

When I think about hearts, the line "In the quiet heart is hidden sorrow that the eye can't see," from the hymn *Lord, I Would Follow Thee* (*Hymns,* no. 220), often comes to mind. In this noisy world we live in, it is hard to notice the sorrow in other people's hearts. Yet it seems that when my heart is aching, burdened, or broken, it hears the quiet hearts around me. When I am aching and just wishing someone would help me, I notice people around me struggling to keep their heads above water. Perhaps this is because I am humbled by my circumstances. And when my heart hurts, I realize how aloof I tend to be to other hurting hearts when I feel good. Clearly, I need to practice "heart listening" on a more regular basis.

One of my favorite verses about hearts is rarely sung in church because it is the fifth verse of a hymn. Unfortunately, most choristers finish the hymn at the end of the fourth verse. The hymn is "Redeemer of Israel," and the verse says, "Restore, my dear Savior, the light of thy face; thy soul cheering comfort impart; And let the sweet longing for thy holy place bring hope to my desolate heart" (ibid, no. 6). I love the imagery of hope conquering a desolate heart.

Here are more lines from hymns: "Dear Lord, prepare my heart to stand with Thee on Zion's mount and never-more to part" ("Let Zion in Her Beauty Rise," ibid, no. 41). "Every day some burden lifted, every day some heart to cheer" ("They, the Builders of the Nation," ibid, no. 36). "An answer comes without a voice; It takes my burden all away and makes my aching heart rejoice" ("Come unto Him," ibid, no. 114). "Thou wilt bind the broken heart . . . enter every timid heart" ("Precious Savior,

Dear Redeemer," ibid, no. 103). "Here bring your wounded heart, here tell your anguish. Earth has no sorrow that Heaven cannot cure" ("Come Ye Disconsolate," ibid, no. 115). This list could go on and on, since many of the hymns deal with matters of the heart.

Hearing and responding to the sound of hearts is life changing. To comfort someone's heart is a blessing. Every heart has a unique heart beat. This means each heart hurts differently and heals differently. When you allow others to be a part of your heart's healing, or when they allow you to be a part of theirs, it is a gift.

THE HEALING HEART

I wish we were as gentle with other people's hearts as God is with ours. How do we deal with loss of love or the pain that love can cause? What about the wounded hearts, the lonely nights, the struggle to allow yourself to love again? What do we do about those who leave us brokenhearted, and those whose hearts we just can't reach? In his book *Making Loss Matter,* Rabbi David Wolpe says:

> *Love is an ever fixed mark in the minds of poets, but in the world, love can fade or end. "Love alters not with his brief hours and weeks," wrote Shakespeare, "but bears it out even to the edge of doom." We want to believe it. But for those who have lost love, the heroic words about everlastingness are mocked by the pain of unhealed hearts. . . . The inescapable paradox of love is this: It is made precious by time, which threatens to*

destroy it. Only through loss can we love, but it is loss that wracks our heart. . . . True love is the outgrowth of the ability to have faith. . . . To love is to accept the possibility of suffering. . . . The root of love is bound up with a knowledge of pain and a consciousness of loss. In the end, such love connects us to God. (1999, 119)

All who love know there is a measure of pain that accompanies it. There is even secondary pain caused by watching someone you care about suffer. But we gladly pick up the broken pieces of our hearts and love again because the alternative is unthinkable. After all, it is the pain that makes us fully aware of the kind of love we have. In his book *The Four Loves,* C.S. Lewis wrote:

To love at all is to be vulnerable. Love anything, and your heart will certainly be wrung and possibly broken. If you want to make sure of keeping it intact, you must give your heart to no one . . . Wrap it carefully round with hobbies and little luxuries; avoid all entanglements; lock it up safe in the casket or coffin of your selfishness . . . the alternative to tragedy, or at least the risk of tragedy, is damnation. The only place outside of Heaven where you can be perfectly safe from all the dangers and perturbations of love is Hell. (1960, 121)

In the end, the choice of who we let guide, inspire, wound, change, and ultimately have our hearts is up to us. If you are given the opportunity to just sit and listen to someone cry, know you are sharing a precious moment. If you are allowed to be in the presence of someone who is struggling with the circumstances that led to his or her broken heart, be sure to appreciate that person's trust. If you are allowed to catch a few fallen tears and bind up a hurting heart, know you are being given a gift from God. These are the moments—raw, naked, and desperate—where lasting friendships and relationships are formed. These precious and rare moments are the makings of great men and women. I treasure the quiet nights when I've shared my room with a grieving soul, when I've sat in silence and listened to heart-wrenching sobs. I treasure the moments when I held my peace and just listened. In those moments—hard as they may be—I realize I would rather love too much than not enough.

Action Questions

- How can you discover the balance between needing to be loved and needing to give more love?
- How can you be more gentle with your heart and the hearts of others?
- Who is currently holding your heart?
- What things can you do (or stop doing) in order to give God more of your heart?
- Are you willing to hear other people's hearts? What can you do to help hurting hearts? How can you help others recognize when your heart is hurting?

SEVEN
Validation

Kindness is the essence of greatness and the fundamental
characteristic of the noblest men and women I have
known. Kindness is a passport that opens doors and fashions
friends. It softens hearts and molds relationships that can last
lifetimes. Kindness is the essence of a celestial life. Kindness is how
a Christlike person treats others. Kindness should permeate
all of our words and actions at work, school, at church, and
especially in our home . . . If you are building others,
you are building the kingdom of God.
—JOSEPH B. WIRTHLIN ("VIRTUE OF KINDNESS," 2005)

You know what it feels like to have someone give you a
compliment just when you need it. Someone who hasn't seen
you in a few weeks says you look like you've lost a lot of weight.
Little did she know you skipped the gym a few too many times
lately and feel fat. Timing is everything! A person reads a story
you've written and gives you positive feedback. A call comes
when you least expect it to tell you that you matter. A student in
the back of the classroom who rarely talks makes a point to let
you know you are his favorite teacher. A handwritten personal
note lets you know your smile matters. A random stranger tells

you she loves your outfit or hair. A girl notices that her date has opened all her doors, paid for everything, walked her to the door at the end of the night, and been a perfect gentlemen—and she tells him she appreciates him. A boy notices how much effort his date put into getting ready for their date and tells her. These are just a few examples of those never-forgotten moments when someone notices the efforts you make and finds a way to let you know. Sometimes these are tender mercies, and sometimes they are just natural compliments born of occasion, but they are always appreciated.

As humans we have a need to be valued, appreciated, loved, and accepted. We need to know that what we do matters. Sometimes in your desperation for approval you put someone up on a pedestal, and when he or she falls, you realize all you really wanted was to be noticed. Sometimes you connect with someone new and want to tell the person everything, so you do and it's too much, and you realize all you really needed was to feel loved. Often you think or even dream about getting a new job that pays you what you are actually worth, when all you really need is to know that what you are already doing at work makes a difference. You go out and get new clothes, style your hair differently, put on more makeup than usual, pinch your cheeks, put on a pair of heels, and head off to conquer the world. Then you realize your feet hurt, you feel like a clown, and the hairstyle you spent forever on looks like it always does, when all you really needed was for someone to tell you that you're beautiful. You find yourself wanting to tell everyone all the amazing things you've accomplished and what has been happening in your life, but no one cares, and you realize all you need is someone to listen to you.

We are living in a YouTube world. A few years ago I watched a little YouTube clip with my best friend called "Validation." If you have time you should go watch it—really, I mean right now. It seriously changed my life. It is a sixteen-minute clip about the power of validation, how one man smiling and making others smile came full circle and in the end blessed his own life. The part about the clip that strikes me is that at the end—after he has done so many things to validate others—he is finally validated. He responds by saying he had never been told that before. REALLY? How is it possible that someone who goes out of his way to compliment and validate others doesn't get validation in return? And yet you know what I am talking about. Some of the people who need the most validation are those who continuously give it out.

LITTLE RED HEARTS

On a random weekend in San Diego, I was just about ready to walk under the archway of the Gas Lamp District when a painting in the Chuck Jones Gallery caught my attention. So my friends and I walked inside and looked around at all the amazing art, but I was drawn to a certain artist's work. The art hanging in galleries is always way beyond my social-worker budget, but I checked the price tag of my favorite piece and actually found it attainable. I pulled out my cell phone and texted myself the name Fabio Napoleoni. His work had these little red hearts in each painting, and I loved them. He also painted swings and trees and other things I adore. On the bottom of each painting was a little sketch letting the buyer know the painting was an original. When I got home, I got online to find out about Fabio and his art. I discovered that like me, he suffers from severe allergies, and that the little red hearts in his work represent his daughter who was born with a heart defect. Knowing this made me love his work even more. So I wrote him a very personal and sincere message about how his work inspires me. I also told him one day I would own one of his paintings.

I didn't expect him to respond but was excited when he did. He said: "I never thought or intended for my work to hang in galleries and have price tags on them as high as they do. I'm grateful for what has happened for me but at the same time always feel that the true message behind it might be lost . . . until I get an email like yours . . . so THANK YOU!!!"

I was glad my message was validation for Fabio—that was enough for me, or so I thought. Then he told me he was going to send me one of his limited-edition art pieces with one of those sketches in the corner. I was ecstatic and had to tell almost every person I know. This experience reconfirmed my belief about the power of sincere, specific compliments and validation.

FIND THE BEST

It is so easy to find what is wrong with the world, people, and situations. Take today, for example. How many times did you think something kind, nice, or positive about yourself? Now compare that to the number of times you thought something negative, deprecating, or false about yourself. The world makes it easy to find fault, to criticize, and to make yourself feel better by putting others down. We all have at least one acquaintance who is always negative and whom we can only handle in small doses, but I wonder if we realize how much negativity we exude.

I am so grateful for a friend years ago who taught me a powerful lesson. One day we were sitting on some steps just talking about life, and she got up the courage to tell me she didn't like hanging around my best friend and me at the same time. I was a little shocked and confused. She explained that although she knew we really cared about each other, we were always negative and sarcastic towards each other. She couldn't understand why, when we had so much in common and really enjoyed spending time together, we would deliberately be so unkind to one another. I was taken aback because I didn't even realize my friend and I acted that way. As a result, I had a candid conversation with my best friend, and we began consciously working on talking with and treating each other according to how we really felt.

This was the beginning of a change for me. I started to notice friends in my life who were negative or who gossiped a lot. I noticed how I felt when I spent time with them. Just recognizing the behavior made me want to have nothing to do with it. I found myself slowly walking away from friendships based on sarcasm or negativity and being drawn to friendships based on honesty and humor.

Finding the best in others or in situations can be easy, but I think it takes practice. I don't think we are naturally inclined to see the best; instead, we tend to see what is wrong. Think about the people in your life who seem to stand out in a good way. What do they all have in common? My guess is they are refreshing and fun to be around because they are positive, full of energy, kind, and validating. People who look for the best in others and in situations eventually start to find the best in themselves. When they find the best in themselves, they are ready to give the best.

Right after my friend pointed out my sarcastic behavior, I decided to change some things in my life. I remember standing in line at a grocery store and this women a few people ahead of me in line had the most beautiful red hair I had ever seen. I remember thinking, *Well, it does no good to her or anyone else if you just think it and don't say anything.* So even though it was a bit awkward, I tapped her on the shoulder and told her I thought she had beautiful hair. She didn't fudge or fuss or deny my compliment—in fact, she smiled and said thank you. That was the beginning of the change for me. I figured I could start changing by vocalizing compliments instead of just thinking them. After I got use to doing that, I started to write little notes to people whenever they came to my mind. One day in high school I was walking down the hall, and as usual people would say, "How are you doing?" They weren't expecting a response—they were saying it more as a form of hello—but I chose to answer uncharacteristically. I would say, "I am fantastic, how are you?" or I would say, "Today is going to be one amazing day!" People would stop or turn around and smile or laugh at the unexpected response.

Once you start giving people sincere, specific compliments, it becomes more natural and instinctive. Also, I have found that when the Lord knows you are willing to share your love and positive affirmations, He will place people in your life or in your heart that you can reach. For a few years now, I have carried around with me a set of notecards of some sort. In my down time, I pull out the cards and write thank-you notes to people—notes of appreciate or validation. Often the Spirit inspires me to write a note to someone who I later find out really needed to hear that someone was thinking of him or her. The same can be done with a quick text, email, or Facebook message.

LISTEN

One of my favorite kinds of validation is simply to listen. On the cork board in my office, there is a sticky note with the acronym "LMTL" written in black marker. For a long time, in addition to that reminder, I had the acronym written in pen on my hand to remind me to "listen more, talk less." I wrote it on my hand to remind me every time I saw it, but also because I knew people would ask me what it meant and I could tell them about the idea of listening more and talking less. This is just one of the ways I have tried to learn to listen more. I have always been a talker. You really can't blame me, since I am from a family of eight children and have five talkative sisters. In my family you either talk, and talk loud, or you don't get anything. I don't remember exactly when it happened, but at one point in my life I realized I needed to make a concerted effort to listen more and talk less.

SEEK TO UNDERSTAND BEFORE BEING UNDERSTOOD

This idea—listening and trying to understand others before your point, opinion, or ideas are voiced—is a very difficult principle to master. Sometimes when I am explaining this idea it is easier to explain to people what it is not. So I share something I like to call the Splat Theory. It is exactly like it sounds. When I am angry or trying to get my point across, I am splatting on you. You don't like me splatting on you, so what do you do? You splat on me, of course. So there we are splatting on each other and getting nowhere.

Another theory I talk about is the Sea Anemone Theory. If you have seen a sea anemone, you know they are beautiful and fascinating to watch, but the moment you poke one to feel it, it clamps shut. It no longer feels safe. Often when we are trying to communicate with others, we poke around to get our ideas, feelings, views, and opinions across.

Seeking to understand before being understood will change every relationship you have. This means you listen before you talk. I challenge you, for an entire day, to apply this principle in every interaction. You will find it is an amazing communication tool.

There have been many times in my life when I wish I hadn't said something, but I have rarely regretted taking the time to listen. There are far too many people who want to talk, and not nearly enough people who are willing to listen. It is amazing the things you learn, not just about others but about yourself, when you take the time to listen.

Validation is so needed in our society. In both my personal life and my professional life, I have been amazed at how motivating a little validation can be. People are starving for attention, and as the saying goes, the grease goes to the squeaky wheel. Often, those who are doing their jobs efficiently and making things happen in their lives are those who get lost in the shuffle of their wards and who rarely receive validation. To those people—and to everyone, for that matter—a few kind words can make a big difference.

Listening more than you talk; seeking to understand before you are understood; finding the best in people, places, and situations; and giving and receiving sincere, specific validation is life changing.

Action Questions

- Who are ten people with traits you admire? Why do you admire these particular people? How can you express that admiration to them?
- Invite someone to watch the YouTube clip *Validation* with you and see what he or she thinks about it.
- How can you go out of your way to give someone a sincere, specific compliment?
- What can you do to become a better listener?
- How can you accept validation when you need it most?
- What can you do to find the best in others, your job, your family, your friends, and your circumstances?

EIGHT

Love-Inspired Change

More fierce desire to stand against the wind
More blazing fire when dark is closing in
A more love-inspired change within
So there's more and more of me to give.
—KENNETH COPE ("MORE," © 2005)

As single adults, we all struggle with self-doubt. While many of our friends get married and move on with life, it is easy to doubt ourselves. We begin to wonder, What is wrong with me? We ask, Am I too fat? What do I need to do in order to date? Am I just not good looking enough? and many other self-deprecating and unproductive questions. Our self-image can be riddled with negativity.

Married people, in their zeal for us to join them in their bliss, start asking us why we're not dating or married. They try to either diagnose the reasons we are single or justify them. Either way, it is hard not to internalize this outside feedback. We start to wonder how and if we can change to improve our situation. For most people, change of any kind is difficult. Sometimes we are doing fine and just need to be patient, but there are times when we need love-inspired change.

THE LETTER CHALLENGES

I would like to share two experiences that significantly impacted my life. Both involved letters, people I hand-picked, a willingness to change on my part, and startling discoveries along the way. Both of these experiences could be called "letter challenges," but each brought about a different love-inspired change in me.

Challenge One: How I See Others

At the end of my junior year of high school, my dad decided to go back to school to get his PhD. We were moving out of state, and I would attend a different high school for my senior year. As happy as I was for my father, I was devastated that I wouldn't graduate with the friends I'd grown up with.

I wanted to do something to remember my last few weeks of school with my friends, and I got this idea. It started in seminary while my teacher was talking to us about being Christlike. I had always struggled with what that means. I could read about Christ, but I always felt that without seeing Him it was hard to understand what it would feel or look like to be like Him. Sitting in class, I decided I would choose different people at school—Mormon or not, friends and strangers—who each exemplified a certain attribute of Christ. I would observe each person for a week and try to emulate that specific attribute, and then I would write the person a letter. There were seven weeks of school left, so I picked seven people and seven attributes. The first week I picked a guy who was a great friend to everyone. I didn't know exactly what made him a good friend, but he was known for his loyalty and friendship. I watched him all week at school, after school, etc. Of course I did all this without him knowing. At the end of the week, it was remarkable how much I had learned about him. I learned very quickly that one of the main reasons he was a great friend is because he was always willing to listen. He spent time with people and had a desire to really understand them. He was aware of those who were lonely and reached out to them. He made an effort to speak positively of others, and he distanced himself from gossip.

When it came time to write him a letter, I was so excited. I thanked him for being a great example and friend to so many. I pointed out specific things I had learned from watching him throughout the week. I explained how much I appreciated his kindness and the impact his listening had on my life. I didn't sign the letter, and I put it in his locker.

I don't know what that letter, or any of the other seven letters, meant to the recipients, but I can tell you this—those seven letters and seven weeks changed my life. By watching friends and even strangers, I learned a great deal about Christlike attributes and how to apply them in my life. I came to better understand my Savior, and I caught a glimpse of how it feels to be like Him.

Challenge Two: How Others See Me

Years ago, I felt I was ready to make whatever changes were necessary to become a better person. With the Lord's help, I had already been working on many of the weaknesses I knew I had, but I was ready for a little more. One day with a prayer in my heart, I wrote a letter. In this letter, I asked the recipient to think about his or her relationship with me. I asked him or her to share with me anything he or she thought would help me to be a better person, improve my dating opportunities, or allow me to progress. I closed by asking the person to pray about the critical feedback he or she should offer, before responding to my letter.

Then I chose ten people, male and female, from various areas of my life. A few were older than me and some were younger. I chose former boyfriends, family members, best friends, and coworkers—people who had spent a significant amount of time with me and knew me well. The most important thing was that I could trust each of the ten people who would receive my letter. I hoped they would know I was serious, that I was ready to hear their criticism, and that I was willing to humble myself in order to change.

A few people immediately responded, but I had to convince the rest that this was very important to me. It is hard for people to share critical things about someone they love. Eventually I received ten responses. Of course, each was unique and from a different perspective, yet each was filled with love. I'd like to say it was easy to read those letters, but it wasn't. Some of the weaknesses I already knew about and was working on, and with other things I had no clue. People are always willing to tell you how you should change, but getting critical feedback that is *love inspired* makes all the difference. I am eternally grateful for the opportunity these ten people gave me to change things about myself in order to become a better person. Those ten letters have made a tremendous impact on my life.

Now a warning: Please do not attempt this kind of challenge unless you are prepared and ready to receive critical freedback from others. I certainly wouldn't recommend this challenge to everyone.

AFTER ALL YOU CAN DO

What if you have done all you can do, and it doesn't seem to be enough? You have tried to be more attractive, you study the scriptures diligently, you serve others, you ask your friends and trusted leaders for help—and yet you remain single. Many Church leaders and seminary and institute teachers spend a great deal of time counseling with singles. I have participated in many of those heartfelt, pleading conversations. I have looked into the eyes of leaders and parents who love me but can't help me because, like me, they don't know why I'm not married.

I am sure you've been told to become the kind of person you want to marry. You've undoubtedly been assured that someday, maybe in the next life, you will be married and receive all the blessings God has promised you. While I believe these statements are true, they don't necessarily comfort me or give me hope for the present. I do have hope for the future, and I know that God loves me and wants to bless me. But I also know that in some ways, whether or not I marry is out of my control.

In many conversations with my single friends, the topic of attraction comes up. To this point, when people want to set me up on a blind date, I usually ask them to have the guy check out my Facebook profile. If he finds me attractive, I'll go out with him. I have learned, as most of you have, that attraction is VERY important. Attraction gets members of the opposite sex to notice each other and to want to get to know each other better.

Because of this fact, many of my single friends focus a lot of their energy on their physical appearance. They see that skinny, beautiful, tan girls and tall, muscular, good-looking guys get married. If singles don't fit into either of these categories, they seem to lose hope that they will ever get married. They spend much of their time and money trying to make themselves look and feel better. If they are honest, they will admit they do all this in the hopes of attracting a spouse. Yet no matter how hard they work to improve themselves physically, these single adults are never completely happy with the results.

If you think your looks are keeping you from dating or getting married, you should definitely do all you can to feel and look better. You have to be willing to pay the price of hard work if you are going to use this as your excuse or comfort. However—and this is important—there is a balance in all things. Too much going to the gym, dieting, tanning, etc., is not good and probably won't get you any closer to finding a spouse. Physical appearance is important in attracting someone of the opposite sex, but it is who you are that keeps a person in a relationship with you. If you do all you can, working on both your inward self and your outward self, you can rest assured that you have done your part.

Some of you are saying right now, "But I have done all I can. I've been working out, eating well, serving, growing spiritually, etc., and I'm still not dating or married." I know how you feel! I think there is a reason why, after all we can do, we still feel there is something missing in our life. No matter how hard we try, no matter what we do to build the kingdom, and no matter how many people love and support us, we are still not 100% happy. I think it is because it is not God's plan for us to be alone in this life. You can take comfort in that. Do your best, hold on to hope, look to the future, and trust in a God who you know loves you dearly.

I believe in the power of change—in fact, I believe in it so much that I chose a career that centers around that focal point. As a social worker, the first and most important lesson I had to learn was that while I can be a broker of resources or an agent of change, I will never be able to *make* people change. Change comes from within. Many times in my life I have wanted to force change upon others. If you have served a mission or watched a loved one make foolish choices, you can relate. But we all know that in order to change, a person has to *want* to change. Bringing about change in your life is hard and doesn't happen overnight, but its effects can be empowering and life-altering.

Action Questions

- How can you get honest feedback to help you make needed changes in your life?
- How can you help your friends and family members make positive changes in their lives?
- What do you want to change about your life? How can you go about making those changes?
- How can you be more patient with yourself? In what ways can you be more gentle and less self-deprecating?

NINE

No Fear

We live in a time of turmoil. Earthquakes and tsunamis wreak devastation, governments collapse, economic stresses are severe, the family is under attack, and divorce rates are rising. We have great cause for concern. But we do not need to let our fears displace our faith. We can combat those fears by strengthening our faith . . . Why do we need such resilient faith? Because difficult days are ahead. Rarely in the future will it be easy or popular to be a faithful Latter-day Saint. Each of us will be tested.
—RUSSELL M. NELSON ("FACE THE FUTURE," 2011)

One day, my friend Seth took my roommate Marie and me to a special spot of his in East Boston. We drove very fast in his convertible Spider with the top down. Once we got to East Boston, the water was beautiful and so was the view of Boston. Seth noticed the tide had risen, so some of the rocks to walk out at this certain spot were covered with water (this should have been our first clue). Marie was wearing flip-flops and had started to roll up her pants to walk out to this rock hill that protruded from the water. Seth and I followed, taking off our socks and stuffing them into our shoes. Once we got to the rock hill, we sat there for a long time, talking and looking out at the harbor and Boston. It was early April, and it started to get cold. When we turned around, we realized the rocks leading back to the shore were now underwater. We could still find the rocks, but they were slippery and the water was cold. After a few minutes of trying to make it back to shore, Seth and I realized our shoes were gone. They were floating away in the water. At this point I was soaking wet, so it just made sense to swim out and rescue our shoes. I looked at the shore, back to where our shoes were, and then back to the shore, hoping I wouldn't get hypothermia. So there I was swimming in the Boston Harbor at 12:30 AM, rescuing our shoes. Mind you it was freezing, but it was so funny. At that moment I was fearless. Looking back, it seemed like such a stupid thing to do for some dumb shoes, but at the time I just jumped in—literally.

Every time I wear those shoes, I smile and think of my swim in the harbor. How often in our lives are we fearless? We tend to be afraid of what others think, afraid we might do something wrong, afraid to put ourselves out there, and afraid of rejection. But we weren't always that way. Do you remember how fearless you were as a kid? Kids jump out of trees thinking they will fly, let go of the wall in the pool thinking they will just float, and run across busy streets like they are invincible. There is something inside of us that changes when we grow up. We lose our invincibility, which is a good thing for safety's sake, but we also gain a great sense of fear.

FEAR VERSUS FAITH

Our fears hinder us from so many things in life, because when we are full of fear we cannot be full of faith. Fear and faith cannot coexist. Many times in the scriptures, the Lord teaches people to let go of fear and to rely on faith instead. Enoch asks the Lord, "Why is it that I have found favor in Thy sight, and am but a lad and all the people hate me; for I am slow of speech; wherefore am I thy servant?" (Moses 6:31). Similarly, Moses tells the Lord, "I am not eloquent, neither heretofore, nor since Thou hast spoken unto thy servant: but I am slow of speech, and of a slow tongue" (Exodus 4:10). And Jeremiah cries, "Ah, Lord God! behold, I cannot speak: for I am a child" (Jeremiah 1:6). These are just three examples of righteous individuals who feared but who went on to do great things for the Lord. They became instruments in His hands—*after* they overcame their fears and moved forward in faith.

During Jesus Christ's ministry, He blessed many people for being full of faith. In Matthew, we read of a leper who said to the Lord, "Lord, if thou wilt, thou canst make me clean" (v. 3). Jesus healed him "immediately" (v. 4). The next story is of a centurion who tells the Lord that one of his servants is grievously ill. When the Lord replies that He will go and heal the servant, the centurion says, "Lord, I am not worthy that thou shouldst come under my roof: but speak the word only, and my servant shall be healed" (Matthew 8:8). Jesus answered, "I have not found so great faith, no not in Israel" (v. 10). In the next chapter, we read the story of the woman who was "diseased with an issue of blood twelve years" (Matthew 9:20). She said within herself, "If I may touch his garment, I shall be whole" (v. 21). When she touched His hem, Jesus felt strength leave Him, and He said to her, "Daughter, be of good comfort; thy faith hath made thee whole" (v. 22). There are many other stories of people who were fearless and full of faith. The scriptures teach us that if we are to expect miracles—if we want to be healed and made whole—we must banish our fears and exercise our faith.

Whether we are single or not, fear can keep us from making decisions. Fear seems to creep in and fill us with indecision, or a false sense of contentment and a feeling that mediocrity is good enough. We reach a point in our lives when we have to make an important decision, but we are overcome with fear and anxiety, which push aside our faith and almost paralyze us. We must continually work and pray to have faith instead of fear, especially when it comes to making decisions.

MAKING DECISIONS

We make thousands of decisions every day. Some of these we don't notice because we make them instinctively, while others are more complicated and obvious. While decision-making is not unique to single people, it certainly can plague us. Many times, in the face of an important decision, I've wanted someone to help me make the decision. Better yet, I wanted someone to just make my decision for me! But that is not God's plan.

We all have so many decisions to make, such as whom to date, whom to marry, which school to attend, where to go to grad school, which job to accept, and so forth. Some decisions will not make much of a difference in our lives, but others will affect eternity. It is no wonder decision-making is so complicated. There are many general conference talks, *Ensign* articles, and books about making decisions. It seems everyone has different ideas as to the best way to effectively make decisions.

The Process

In the Church, the process we hear about most involves studying the issue in your mind, making your own decision, and then asking the Spirit to confirm your choice if it is right.

But, behold, I say unto you, that you must study it out in your mind; then you must ask me if it be right, and if it is right I will cause that your bosom shall burn within you; therefore, you shall feel that it is right.

But if it be not right you shall have no such feelings, but you shall have a stupor of thought that shall cause you to forget the thing which is wrong. (Doctrine and Covenants 9:8–9)

This passage of scripture teaches us how to not only make a decision but how to approach God once we've made the decision. The "it" in these two verses is the question or the decision you are making. Simply stated, you need to study out your question, make a decision, ask God to confirm your decision, and wait for His answer. If your decision is right, He will cause you to *feel* that it is right, and if it is wrong He will cause you to have a stupor of thought. It sounds very easy, but it can be difficult in practice.

Often when we make decisions, we don't do our part before we go to the Lord and seek His help. We want to skip the studying part and go straight to the asking part. This isn't usually how the Lord works. We need to figure out what to ask for, narrow down our options, brainstorm, do some studying and pondering—maybe over a long period of time—and make a decision. Once we have done our part, we can go to the Lord and ask Him to confirm or reject our decision. Making decisions is much more than getting on our knees and asking the Lord to answer our questions. We need to have faith that if we follow the process outlined in the Doctrine and Covenants, the Lord will eventually confirm our decisions. Although using our agency, making decisions, and following through with those decisions is sometimes difficult, not making a much needed decision can also prove challenging.

One day I was called into my mission president's office. I was extremely nervous—I felt like I was back in high school and had been called into the principal's office. It's never a good thing being called to the office. I walked in, sat down, and looked at the president. I could see he was troubled, and I wondered if something bad had happened to one of my family members. He said nothing was wrong with me or my family, but that he wanted me to do something for him. With a heavy heart, he asked me to go talk to two sister missionaries who were having a difficult time and wanted to go home. I couldn't fathom wanting to go home because I had wanted to serve a mission since I was ten years old and was trying to squish eleven years of anticipation into eighteen short months. My mission president explained his concern for the sisters and asked me to meet with them. He told me to do whatever was necessary to help the sisters understand the importance of their role as missionaries, to try to convince them to stay. If they were still set on going home early, he would meet with them for their final interview. This was a daunting task for me. I could understand if an elder didn't want to be on his mission, because elders were there by commandment. But at that point I couldn't understand why sister missionaries would choose to come on a mission and then not want to stay.

I asked the Lord to open my mind and heart to what these sister missionaries were feeling. My companion and I drove to the first sister's apartment and knocked on the door. My companion and the companion of the sister who wanted to go home left and went to some teaching appointments. As I walked into the apartment and sat down on the couch, I could feel a heaviness in the air. I asked the struggling sister to offer a prayer. She declined, so I prayed for both of us. Then we talked about how things were going for her. She started complaining right away about how the elders in her district hated her, how her companion was lazy, and how all their appointments canceled or the people weren't home when the sisters showed up. She complained about having to ride a bike in a dress, having to spend all her time with her companion, and a myriad of other things. At this point, even I was ready for her to go home! She didn't appreciate or value any of the things a mission had to offer, and in my opinion she was being very selfish.

Just before it was my turn to speak I could see, in my mind's eye, my mission president's face, full of love and concern for this sister. The Spirit testified to me that this sister needed to stay on her mission, not only for herself but for her family. I was a little surprised at the clarity and forcefulness with which the Spirit impressed these things on my mind. I felt inspired to simply ask this sister, "Why did you decide to go on a mission?" She told me how she hadn't wanted to serve a mission but was sitting in church one day and a returned missionary was giving his homecoming talk. She told me how the Spirit very strongly told her she needed to serve a mission, and that is why she came. She said she had never wanted to serve a mission but that God told her to come, through the Spirit, so she did.

As she spoke, all I could think of was that maybe she needed to decide to *be* on a mission—that even though she was already serving, she still needed to make the conscious decision to be there. She had never made the decision herself; she had let the Spirit move her and had gone through the motions, but never made the personal commitment. That is why when things got tough she had nothing to fall back on. I shared with her my impressions from the Spirit and watched as her heart changed. She started to cry and confided in me that the mission was so much harder than she had anticipated. I shared with her some of my own struggles, and in the end she knew she needed to stay. We talked about how things could be different for her on her mission. We did a little problem-solving and set up an appointment to talk to her district leaders.

Before I left, I asked this missionary if she thought it was important to decide, for herself, to serve a mission. She said yes, and we read Doctrine and Covenants 9:8–9 and talked about the importance of making decisions. Then, she got on her knees and did what most missionaries do well before they get their mission call. She asked God if serving a mission was the right decision at this time for her. She told Him she had a desire to serve but needed His help to get through the hard days. When she finished, the Spirit was very strong in the apartment, and the sister had tears streaming down her face. This time she had decided to serve a mission, had it confirmed through the Spirit, and knew that although it would hard, she could make it.

As I left the apartment, I was so grateful that the Spirit had guided me to the right question to ask that sister missionary. Our discussion could have gone in many different directions, and if it had been up to me at first I would've handed her a ticket home. But the Lord knew her heart. He knew what questions she needed to be asked and the decision she needed to make.

The Right Questions

A critical part of making a decision is starting with the right question. Often, we are most concerned with the answer or outcome rather than finding the right question. For instance, let's say you are dating two different girls and like both of them for different reasons. It's time to decide which one to break up with and which one to keep dating. You are struggling with your decision so you go to the Lord for help. What is the question you ask Him? Do you kneel down and ask, "Can you please help me know which girl I should choose to date?" What if you have applied to many different grad schools and are wondering which school you should go to. Do you ask God, "Which school should I go to?" What if you are contemplating buying a house. Do you ask the Lord, "Should I buy a house?"

While all of these questions are good, they are not specific enough. Rarely will the Lord answer, "You should date Catherine not Camille," "Arizona State University is the grad school for you," or "Yes, buy a house and make sure it is located in Newport Beach, California." If you do receive these kind of answers, you are blessed—and I need to figure out what you are doing! If you are like most people, specific answers don't come in response to vague questions. Figuring out the right question takes time and effort. Saying to Heavenly Father, "I have thought a lot about buying a house, and I have saved money for a long time. I feel I am ready for this big responsibility. I found a great realtor, looked at lots of different houses, and feel that the house in Newport Beach is the right one for me. Is this the right house for me at this time?" is much more specific than asking, "Should I buy a house?"

Making decisions with faith and without fear takes work and is a process. If you can ask the right question from the beginning, the decision-making process will be much easier.

Action

Once you have figured out the right question and completed your decision-making process, it is time to act upon your decision. This part can be easier said than done. Sometimes it feels as if you are stepping into the darkness or moving forward with no guarantee of success. Other times, acting on decisions feels great. For me, it is often difficult to turn a decision into action. According to scripture, I am not alone in this difficulty. As we look at a couple of Bible stories, it is important to notice the point where a decision plus faith turns into action, and where action becomes a miracle.

The story of the children of Israel always fascinated me as a kid—the plagues, the crossing of the Red Sea, the wandering in the wilderness, the manna from heaven, the bitter water that was healed, the golden calf. I marveled at the Lord's bounteous blessings on His people even when they were foolish and murmured after 430 years of pleading to be delivered from bondage. I'd read this story many times, but one day as I was preparing to teach a seminary class in Boston, one phrase in Exodus jumped out at me. There are many powerful and beautiful phrases in chapter 14, but this wasn't any of those. This particular verse reads: "And the Lord said unto Moses, Wherefore criest thou unto me? speak unto the children of Israel, that they go forward" (Exodus 14:15).

Immediately I thought of Simon Peter in Matthew 14:22–33. When we study this passage of scripture, we usually talk about Peter and his walking on the water—how his faith falters and the Lord saves him. But I was drawn to a different part of the story: "And when Peter was come down out of the ship . . ." With the children of Israel and with Peter, action (faith plus works) had to be taken before the miracles occurred. The children of Israel had to walk toward the Red Sea before Moses parted it by the Lord's power. Peter had to get out of the boat and step onto the water before he could walk toward the Savior.

I wonder how many times in my life I have pleaded with the Lord for deliverance, or for Him to make decisions for me. Then as He made it happen, in His time and on His terms, I have murmured because the way seemed impossible. How many times have I come to a decision but lacked the faith to turn it into action? I wonder how often I've asked the Lord to work miracles in my life, but when the opportunity came I sat inside the boat instead of stepping out onto the water.

Many times, we are paralyzed by fear and failure, and our progress is hindered by our inability to make critical decisions. Now is the time to be more of a believer and less of a murmurer.

It is time to make decisions—to act—and watch the Lord work miracles in our lives. We need to spend more time walking through the Red Sea and walking on the water of the Sea of Galilee, and less time standing on dry ground or sitting in the boat.

"It Had Been Better . . ."

We've discussed making and following through with important decisions, but what happens *between* those decisions? While I have my fair share of struggles with the decision-making process, I seem to struggle much more with having patience through all the "wandering" in the wilderness before I reach my destination. I was sitting in Sunday School one day, and the teacher was talking about the children of Israel. I was thinking, "Yeah, yeah. They wander, they complain, they get blessed, they wander more, they complain, and so forth." Then the teacher posed the question "What lessons can we learn from the children of Israel?" It wasn't a difficult question and everyone seemed to know the typical answers, but the question evoked inside of me a realization I hadn't been willing to confront. I was no better than the children of Israel!

I thought about my life before my mission and how I wandered around, trying to figure out what to do with my life, what to major in, where I should work, where to live, and on and on. I remember complaining to the Lord and asking what direction I should go and what and where I needed to be. It took some time—and some excruciating trials of faith—but the way appeared and I was on the path. I declared a major, found great friends, and served a mission. Life was grand.

Then I graduated and was again faced with what to do and where to go with my life. So I began to wander and complain to the Lord. This time I wandered longer, the way was harder, and the questions were much more desperate. I didn't know what to do with my life, where to live, where to work, and I had so many unanswered questions about why my life wasn't working out the way I had planned. I felt the Lord had closed all the doors, and I needed Him to open a window. Like the children of Israel I lacked faith, yet in the midst of my complaining and heartfelt desire to do God's will, He opened a window like manna from heaven. I moved to Boston and began my life there. I loved every minute I was in Boston.

It didn't take long however, before the wandering began again. I started murmuring about maybe starting a career, maybe settling down and getting married. It was my turn for good things to happen, I thought. Suddenly I began to feel lost again, wishing I could just go back to the days when I was happy. Then the Lord, line by line, precept upon precept, guided me to graduate school. So off I went to the desert of Arizona. There I literally walked in the desert, only this time, for a few years, I wasn't wandering. I had a solid two-year plan and I loved it.

I figured I would get my master's degree, find a job in my career, and be on my way in life. That's how it works, right? Well, like the children of Israel, I hadn't learned my lesson. It had only been ten years of wandering, not forty, yet once again the cycle began. I graduated with my master's degree and desperately tried to find a job in my field. I murmured and complained and bargained with the Lord. I asked Him why I had been directed to get a master's degree if I wasn't going to be able to get a job in that field. I waited, and waited, and pled, and complained, and waited some more. The answers didn't come, and there I was sitting in the Sunday School class being asked if I could relate to the children of Israel.

I chuckled, took a deep breath, and recognized my lack of faith. Surely, just as the Lord had blessed the children of Israel all along, He had done the same for me. I had been living my life just like the children of Israel. When they were approaching the Red Sea and could see and hear the Egyptians chasing after them, their faith faltered and they were overcome with fear. They said, "For it had been better for us to serve the Egyptians, than that we should die in the wilderness" (Exodus 14:12). Here they are on the brink of a miracle and they want to go back to Egypt as slaves! The Israelites were always looking back in fear of the future and longing for the miserable past. They lacked the faith they needed to allow the Lord to take care of them and lead them to the promised land.

I don't know how many years you have been wandering or where exactly your wilderness is, but I know it can get lonely out there. And while I don't have the answers, I know God does. He provided everything the children of Israel needed, and He will provide for you not only what you need but also what you desire in righteousness. Have faith, look to the future, and know that while you may wander for a while, eventually you will find the promised land. And it will be well worth the journey.

Action Questions

- What decisions in your life are you not making because of fear?
- How can you show more faith in your life?
- Are there decisions in your life that you need to turn into action?
- In what ways can you start looking and walking forward instead of longing for the past?

TEN
Wolf's Law

I heard the Prophet Joseph Smith say to the Twelve,
"You will have all kinds of troubles and trials to pass through.
And it is quite as necessary for you to be tried, even as
Abraham and other men of God." And said he, "God will feel
after you and he will take hold of you and wrench your very heart
strings. And if you cannot stand it, you will not be fit for
an inheritance in the Celestial Kingdom of God."
—JOHN TAYLOR (IN *JOURNAL OF DISCOURSES,* 1884, 24:197)

A friend introduced me to Wolf's Law, a theory developed by German anatomist and surgeon Julius Wolf. In the nineteenth century, he developed the theory that bones in a healthy person or animal will adapt to the loads they are placed under. When weight or pressure on a particular bone increases, the bone will remodel itself over time to become stronger to resist that weight. Basically, the more weight you place on a bone, the more dense it becomes and the more able to support the added weight.

This applies in many different areas of life. Tennis players get denser bones in their racquet-holding arms. Surfers get "surf knots" on their knees from paddling out into the ocean.

Teenagers' bones can endure more stress because they are more actively applying pressure to their bones than their grandparents are. Gymnasts apply so much pressure to their bones that it actually affects how they grow. One of the reasons older adults' bones become brittle is because older adults are less active and therefore put less pressure or weight on their bones. This causes their bones to decrease in density. When there is no weight or pressure on a bone, it atrophies. Astronauts return from space and find their bones are less dense. The more the weight or pressure on a bone, the stronger it becomes.

It's the same thing with life. Adversity and trials give us opportunities to become stronger. Some of the people I admire and look up to the most have endured tragedy, heartache, or some other kind of life-changing trial. After they endured the trial—after the pressure or weight set in on their souls—they had the ability to endure subsequent trials with renewed strength. They are better, wiser, more compassionate, more humble, more willing to listen, and closer to the Lord because of the burdens they've borne. I am attracted to people who are acquainted with grief, who know what it means to fall on their knees in desperation, and who have stood on the brink and have chosen God. They are warriors, and I am grateful and in awe in their presence.

Whenever someone talks about trials or adversity, a scripture from the war chapters in the Book of Mormon comes to my mind.

But behold, because of the exceedingly great length of the war between the Nephites and the Lamanites [cause] many had become hardened [effect], because of the exceedingly great length of the war; and many were softened [effect] because of their afflictions [cause], insomuch that they did humble themselves before God, even in the depth of humility [effect]. (Alma 62:41)

The same causes, the "great length of the war" and the related afflictions, brought about such dramatically different results. Many people's hearts were hardened as a result of the war and the subsequent afflictions, but other people's hearts were softened and humbled. How is it possible for the same trials to cause such different results? Each heart will be uniquely tested. Will you have a hard heart or a humble heart?

A few days after my brother died, our house was filled with people wandering in and out. I remember sitting in the living room, staring at our kitchen counter, which was covered with food. In fact, the food was rotting because there was no room in the fridge and no one was really in the mood to eat. In addition, there were flowers all over the house, but they were dying and wilting. I sat there thinking that what we really needed was someone to come and throw away the dead flowers and the rotting food. Instead the food kept coming and so did the flowers. I was full of anger toward people who didn't notice these things, which were obvious to me. I was tired of hearing people say stupid things that certainly weren't comforting. My heart was anything but humble.

At that moment, I got a phone call from a friend. She had heard about my brother and wanted to give her support. Her advice has stayed with me. She said that if ever there was a time for me to yell, scream, swear, or throw a tantrum, now would be that time. I laughed. Right there in a room full of dreary, devastated people and dying flowers and rotting food—I laughed. And in that laugh I felt free. I was humbled by my friend's willingness to be still in her busy life and listen to the Spirit's prompting to call me. She didn't offer me clichéd accolades. She didn't talk to me about how she got through her mother's long years of suffering and then dying from cancer. She didn't tell me that everything was going to work out or that my brother was in a better place. She listened, loved me, and supported me. I owe her so much for that phone call and what it did to change my perspective that day.

When I was twenty-five and living in Provo, Utah, I had another life-changing experience. One day, a mentor of mine basically told me I could do anything I wanted. She asked me to think about my possibilities instead of focusing on my limitations. I wanted to be in a healthy, fun relationship heading towards marriage. I wanted to be a mother. I wanted to be anything but single with no plans for my future. My mentor asked me where I would live if I could live anywhere I wanted, and I said the East Coast. She said, "Make it happen." Those three words changed my life. Being single had seemed like a burden or trial, but all of a sudden it was freeing and simple. I could just up and move if I wanted, so I did. As stated before, I joined AmeriCorps and moved to Boston, and that was just the beginning of many wonderful opportunities. Our trials often turn out to be some of our greatest blessings.

God understands us, which is why He can help us endure and overcome our trials. While serving in the Relief Society general presidency, Chieko N. Okazaki said:

I don't believe that faith means God will remove all tragedies from our path or solve all our problems for us. I believe it means that He will be with us, suffering with us and grieving with us and working with us as we deal with our own tragedies and work our way through our problems. (Okazaki, *Aloha*, 1995, 119)

Having faith in Christ does not mean we won't suffer. In fact, we *will* suffer. We will be tested. We will endure pain that will cause us to either turn our hearts to God or turn away from Him. These are pivotal moments in our trials, where we stand on the brink of faith, truth, and pain. During these moments, it can seem almost impossible to endure the pain and remain faithful. At the same time, it seems unfathomable to endure the pain without the Spirit. I believe these moments form our character.

THE LAW OF UNDULATION

We all experience trials, adversity, and pain, and like the Lamanites and Nephites, it is up to each of us how we allow those trials to affect us. It is often less about why we are going through a particular trial and more about what we can learn from it.

I love how C.S. Lewis describes trials in *The Screwtape Letters* (1943). The book is about a devil named Screwtape, who writes letters to his nephew, Wormwood, who is training to become a devil. In one letter, Screwtape is describing to Wormwood the "Law of Undulation." Screwtape writes, "Their [humans'] nearest approach to constancy, therefore, is undulation—the repeated return to a level from which they repeatedly fall back, a series of troughs and peaks" (p. 44). In this book the Enemy is God, and Screwtape is trying to teach Wormwood how to win the souls of men and tear them away from God. Screwtape continues, "In [God's] efforts to get permanent possession of a soul, He relies on the troughs even more than on the peaks. Some of His special favorites have gone through longer and deeper troughs than anyone else" (45).

Screwtape goes on to say that God can't always be there for His children, because He can't just override a human's will. "He cannot ravish. He can only woo." This senior devil declares that God does a little "over-riding at the beginning"—"communications of His presence . . . emotional sweetness . . . and easy conquest over temptation" (46). But this will never last long. Screwtape goes on to explain:

Sooner or later [God] withdraws, if not in fact, at least from their conscious experience, all those supports and incentives. He leaves the creature to stand up on its own legs—to carry out from the will alone duties which have lost all relish.

It is during such trough periods, much more than during the peak periods, that it is growing into the sort of creature He wants it to be. Hence the prayers offered in the state of dryness are those which please Him best . . . He wants them to learn to walk and must therefore take away His hand; and if only the will to walk is really there He is pleased even with their stumbles. Do not be deceived, Wormwood. Our cause is never more in danger than when a human, no more desiring, but still intending, to do our Enemy's will, looks round upon a universe from which every trace of Him seems to have vanished, and asks why he has been forsaken, and still obeys. (47–48)

There is a power in turning to God that will reverberate throughout every facet of your life. The sooner you learn to rely on Him, the more you will learn and grow. Not that you won't have trials that will test your soul, but you will come to understand what you need to learn from those trials. Turning your heart to God in the peaks of life is great, but even better is turning your heart to him in the troughs.

RIGHTEOUS IN THE DARK

Whenever I get frustrated or don't understand something in Church doctrine, I turn to my dad for advice. Most of the time, he will counsel with me and refer me to a few scriptures or a general conference talk, and then let me find the answers to my own questions. On one particular night, I was feeling very lonely both as a single adult and as a child of God. I remember telling my dad that I felt abandoned by Heavenly Father. I hadn't felt the Spirit in a long time, I didn't feel my prayers were being heard, and I was frustrated at God's silence.

My dad sympathized with me and then introduced me to a principle called "righteous in the dark." This phrase comes from Brigham Young. In talking about trials, his secretary wrote,

President Brigham Young, who knew something about trial and tribulation but also of man's high destiny, said that the Lord lets us pass through these experiences that we might become true friends of God. By developing our individual capacities, wisely exercising our agency, and trusting God—including when we feel forsaken or alone—then we can, said President Young, learn to be "righteous in the dark." (Secretary's Journal, 1857)

It is one thing to be a disciple of Christ when things are going well in your life. It is easy to keep the commandments when you see the correlating blessings. It is something entirely different to remain faithful and loyal to Christ when you are alone in darkness and silence. Henry B. Eyring said:

So, the great test of life is to see whether we will hearken to and obey God's commands in the midst of the storms of life. It is not to endure storms, but to choose the right while they rage. And the tragedy of life is to fail in that and so fail to qualify to return in glory to our heavenly home. (Eyring, "Start Early and Be Steady," 2005)

I allow myself to have hard days, to cry sometimes. Recently on Mother's Day in my family ward, I thought about my wonderful mother. I was smiling and happy. Then, I looked around at all the mothers in my ward and their little children in their arms, and a great sadness washed over me. I want to be a mother. I want to be dragged out to the drinking fountain or bathroom. I want to argue with my husband over whose turn it is to change the diaper. I want those things! So I cried, right there next to my roommates, who understood and just let me. When I was done I wiped away my tears, made sure I didn't have mascara running down my face, and went to Sunday School. There are days when I am surrounded by people but consumed with loneliness. I know I am not alone in these feelings. Some say that being single is a trial, and others say it is a blessing. I agree with both. I am grateful I have many more good days than bad days. I am also grateful for tender-mercy moments when the Spirit speaks to my mind and heart and gives me a wider view of God's plan.

A WINDOW'S VIEW

My brother drowned on a Saturday. The following Monday, none of us were really into doing anything family related, so I hoped we would just skip family home evening altogether. But my mother gathered us in the front room and had us look out our big bow window. She asked us to look up, around, and down—to notice everything we could and couldn't see through the window. We had no idea what this was all about, so we just did as we were told. Then she asked us all to go across the street to the abandoned lot. Once we got there, she asked us to again look up, around, and down—to notice what we could and couldn't see. She asked, "Where can you see more?" We went back inside, and my mom taught us a lesson I will never forget. She talked about how in this life we have a limited or window's view of Heavenly Father's ways and His plan. We can see a lot out of our window, but we are limited. Like our view from across the street, Heavenly Father sees a much bigger picture. The concept of this object lesson was so simple and yet so profound. I am grateful for a mother who taught me about a loving God who sees things from a much broader prospective. I am grateful for people who allow me to have bad days. But most importantly I am grateful that through Christ, there is always hope.

DELIVERANCE IS NIGH

I love the lines "There is hope smiling brightly before us, and we know that deliv'rance is nigh," from the hymn "We Thank Thee, O God, for a Prophet" (*Hymns,* no. 19). Something about the word *deliverance* speaks peace to my soul. We all long for some kind of deliverance. We need to know that what we do matters. We need to know there is a plan bigger than us, that we can be happy now. We need to know we are not alone.

Soon after Elder Richard G. Scott's wife died, he gave a talk in general conference titled "Trust in the Lord." I remember his talk vividly because he gave it a few months after my thirty-year-old aunt was killed in a car accident. She left behind my uncle and their four boys, ages nine months to six years. My entire family was devastated and reeling from her unexpected death at such a young age. I have read Elder Scott's talk many times as I struggle through heartache and trials. This apostle of the Lord declares:

> *When the Lord closes one important door in your life, He shows His continuing love and compassion by opening many other compensating doors through your exercise of faith. He will place in your path packets*

of spiritual sunlight to brighten your way. They often come after the trial has been the greatest, as evidence of the compassion and love of an all-knowing Father. They point the way to greater happiness, more understanding, and strengthen your determination to accept and be obedient to His will. (Scott, "Trust in the Lord," 1995)

Heavenly Father gives us little moments, tender mercies, along the way during our trials, as evidence of His love and compassion. I continue to be amazed at the "packets of spiritual sunlight" He places in my path.

I don't know what is weighing on your heart right now, but I imagine it is heavy and that no matter how many people are supporting you, you feel lonely. Maybe you have lost hope in the dating scene. Maybe you are still heartsick over a messy divorce. Maybe you are tired of watching everyone you know get married. Maybe you are sick of getting wedding announcements or birth announcements. Maybe you are tired of everyone's advice as to why you aren't married yet. Maybe you are aching for the touch of another person. Maybe you are longing for someone to talk to about your day—someone who is invested in you. Or maybe, just maybe, you are one of those single people out there that is happy with life but still feels lonely. Whatever your circumstances, whatever trough you might be sludging through, you are not alone. Deliverance is nigh. You can be righteous in the dark, and God will count your tears.

Action Questions

- Write down the Wolf's Law moments that have helped form your character.
- What have you learn about yourself through those trials?
- In what ways can you turn to God more in your life?
- Who are the "warriors" in your life? What can you learn from them about being "righteous in the dark"?
- When you have trials or heartaches, where do you turn your heart?

ELEVEN

Be Still

And Moses said unto the people, Fear ye not, stand still,
and see the salvation of the Lord, Which he will shew
to you today: for the Egyptians whom ye have seen today,
ye shall see them again no more for ever. The Lord shall
fight for you, and ye shall hold your peace.

—EXODUS 14:13–14

Driving to southern Utah to get away for a few days, my roommate and I were singing to music and having a great time. At one point, we slowed down because the road narrowed to one lane in each direction. Ahead of us were a semi-truck and a few cars. We watched in horror as a car tried multiple times to pass the semi-truck. Each time, the car had to speed back into our lane to avoid being hit by oncoming traffic. When the impatient driver finally decided to go for it, he barely got his car in front of the semi without getting hit. I really thought there was going to be a massive collision. Ironically, just after that driver risked so many lives, a passing lane appeared. My friend and I safely passed the semi-truck, as did many of the cars behind us and in front of us, and the kamikaze guy's car ended up right where it had been before—right in front of us.

If there is one thing singles are really good at it is staying busy. I think there is an unspoken fear that if we don't stay busy we might all of sudden realize we are lonely. So we cram our schedules with work, school, church, friends, food (lots of food), entertainment, errands, and so much more. In fact, when we have extra time or space in our schedule it gets gobbled up by TV or Facebook. Don't get me wrong—I know you also go to the temple and to Church activities, and that you date, volunteer, practice your talents, and do a slew of other good things. In this, I think we pack our schedules so full that there is no room to actually reflect, to experience shared moments, to listen to the Spirit, and to truly live with intent.

We live in a nation of instant gratification where our eyes, ears, and hands need to be constantly in motion. It is common to see someone watching TV with a laptop on his or her lap, food next to him or her, and texting on a cell phone. Good luck if you want to actually have a conversation with that person! But in all seriousness, being too busy has become a pandemic for singles.

It wasn't too long ago that a guy would ask a girl out on a date either face to face or over the telephone. Then, on the pre-arranged day, he would pick her up, engage in conversation with her, and buy her a meal, and they would participate together in some sort of activity. At the end of the date, the guy would walk the girl to her door and make sure she got inside safely. Lately I've seen people "date" via text messages, Facebook, or smart phones. While I think most dating today is somewhere in between these scenarios, you probably get what I'm saying about missing the shared moments.

My great-grandmother used to tell me stories of when she was a girl, before there were cars, electricity, television, and even dentists. She would say, "If your tooth was hurting you, we just pulled it out." I enjoyed hearing her adventures with horses, working on the homestead, dances held outside to live music, and how well she knew the people in her community. There is something so magical about being outdoors, sleeping under the stars, dancing to live music, telling stories in the dark, climbing trees, building barns together, walking from one place to the next, and letting each task be enough in itself.

As a missionary, I noticed a distinct difference when my companion and I rode bikes rather than driving a car. When we rode bikes, we could more easily stop and talk to people, whereas in a car we only went to places where we had appointments. We missed so much that was going on outside the car.

BE PRESENT

Today we are excellent multitaskers. In fact, we wouldn't think of leaving the house without our to-do list. If you're like me there's the grocery shopping, picking up the dry cleaning, going to the bookstore, picking up more ink for my printer—and this is all on my way to some activity or on my way home from school or work. Sound familiar?

The idea of being still is a bit foreign to many people. Some think that being still means they are lazy, while others think being still is boring. We are so prone to always be doing something that we miss many precious moments. How often do you process what has happened that day? Do you take inventory of what you have accomplished? I'm not talking about checking items off a list, scolding yourself for what you didn't get done, or making a list of things to do tomorrow. I'm talking about clearing out some negotiable space in your busy, noisy life to be present and listen. It is amazing the things you can hear when you are willing to be still.

ANGRY BIRDS

Over the last few years, I've noticed a trend, especially among teenagers, of a constant need to have some kind of electronic device going at all times. If you are not on your cell phone texting or calling someone, you are probably playing Angry Birds on your phone, listening to music on your MP3 player, or reading a book on your Kindle. One day, I got on the subway in Boston and looked around at the other people. Every single person I could see was either playing with a cell phone or wearing ear phones. I laughed out loud at the sight. Whatever happened to talking to people, to being friendly?

On my mission, the mission president told us we were no longer allowed to listen to any music except hymns. I was devastated. I absolutely love music and knew I would have a hard time with this rule. In one of my interviews, I asked the president why we couldn't listen to other kinds of good music. He explained that music, while it can be good, is usually distracting—it takes away one's focus. He challenged me to turn off the music, even hymns, when my companion and I were driving in our car to appointments and to talk to each other and prepare for our next meeting. I was annoyed but listened to him and found it very difficult at first to get into the car and drive in silence. But over time my companion and I started talking about our upcoming appointments, our feelings about investigators, etc. It soon became apparent that we could feel the Spirit more and communicate better without the distraction of music.

Music, cell phones, hand-held games, laptops, and the like are amazing devices that allow us to accomplish tasks or be entertained. The problem happens when they take the place of actually living real life.

Have you tried riding your bike to work instead of driving? Have you taken a bus instead of driving your car? Have you walked around your neighborhood lately and said hi to your neighbors? When was the last time you read a book—an actual book where you turn real pages and can smell how old it is? What about writing a letter to someone? No, not an email, text, or chat. I'm talking about an actual letter—the kind where you write with a pen, put the letter in an envelope, put a stamp on it, and mail it.

DISCONNECT

With all our technology, life can get hectic, and we need to disconnect once in a while. Have you ever purposely left your phone at home for the day? Have you tried not taking your phone to the gym, on a date, etc? Do you limit the amount of time you spend on Facebook, surfing the web, reading blogs, sending texts? If you have, you know it is much harder than it would seem. Occasionally, I go on what I call a technology fast. This is where I limit my cell phone use, put my iPod away, stay off Facebook, only check my email once a day, and so forth. This gives me a chance to disconnect, be still, and fill that time with other things. The last few times I did a technology fast, many of my friends got upset that I didn't return their texts fast enough, that I didn't respond to their Facebook messages, or that I didn't call them back. I tried to explain why I needed to disconnect from technology for a few days, but it was lost on them.

At times I think we have grown so accustomed to our technology that we don't know what to do once we close the laptop, turn off the phone, pull out the ear buds, and actually enjoy reality. But we simply can't allow technology to take the place of real life and real interactions. Lest you think I don't enjoy all that technology has to offer, I am absolutely in awe of all the devices out there that keep people connected. I love that I can watch TV on Hulu and don't have to even own a television. I love having a cell phone. I am amazed that I can see my niece in Baltimore via Skype and that I can upload and download all sorts of cool things. I love that on my laptop I can create music, record it, add pictures and video clips to it, and create my own movie. While doing all that I write on my blog, write in my journal, listen to iTunes, and update my Facebook status. I love it all but hope to keep the balance.

Another problem with all these helpful devices is that using them all the time leaves us no time for more important things. In Luke, we read about Jesus' visit to his dear friends Mary and Martha, who were sisters. At the end of the story it says, "But one thing is needful: and Mary hath chosen that good part" (Luke 10:42). Cell phones, laptops, e-Readers, MP3 players, cameras, video games, movies, etc., all have their time and place, but if they take the place of needful things, they become a distraction.

Be sure you are out living your life, not rotting behind a TV or a computer screen. During one of my last years at BYU, I was in a fabulous ward and we all lived very close to each other. I really liked my roommates, my classes, and my job. Things were going well except for one area—dating. I wasn't the only one who seemed to be on a dating hiatus. After a few weeks of wondering why none of us girls were getting asked out, I happened upon something. I was over at my guy friends' house and they had two TVs set up in their back room. On each TV there was an Xbox, and four players could play on each Xbox. When I walked in, I saw eight very handsome and eligible young men sprawled over couches and chairs playing Halo. They were excited to tell me about their awesome setup. Come to find out they had actually connected their two Xbox's to two other Xbox's hooked up to two TVs, and there were eight other guys in another house also playing Halo. So, there were sixteen of the coolest, best-looking guys in the ward playing Halo with each other for days on end. They thought it was the best thing ever, but the girls in the ward stopped wondering why no one was getting asked out.

I'm not a gamer, but I'm not against gaming. I just think there is a time and a place for fiction and fun. Life needs to be lived in real moments with real people. Conversations need to take place face to face and not just via text or email. Entertainment is just that—it is meant to entertain, not to take over your real life. Elder Dallin H. Oaks said,

Technology toys like video games and the Internet are already winning away the time of our . . . youth.

> *Surfing the Internet is not better than serving the Lord*
> *or strengthening the family. . . . Some young people are*
> *amusing themselves to death—spiritual death.* (Oaks,
> "Good, Better, Best," 2007)

WHEN THE DAY IS DONE

I have always loved beautiful sunsets. There is something magical about catching the last glimpses of an orange sky filled with pink or purple clouds as the sun begins exchanging places with the moon. As a kid I thought the rain was God's tears, the rainbow was the gift of His love, and the sunsets were His way of saying goodnight to me. I often find myself going a million miles an hour, but I stop in my tracks at the majesty of a sunset. They always make me catch my breath, evaluate my day, and be still. If I could have it my way, every night sky would be filled with a beautiful sunset and everyone would pause at its beauty and take note. How different the world would be.

Wherever I live, I find a place to be still. During my childhood in Oregon, I would hide behind the big lilac bush on the side of our house. In Utah I sit under the tree planted in memory of my brother. In Massachusetts, when I needed to think and get away from the world, I would go to the Old North Bridge. In San Diego I would sit on a bench at Heritage Park next door to the Mormon Battalion Visitor's Center. In Arizona I would walk with a friend of mine down by Tempe Town Lake. These places and more are special to me because they are safe, peaceful, free from the world, and simple. In these places, like the temple, I take a step away from the world, technology, drama, and stress, and step into stillness.

Take an inventory of how you spend your in-between time. What do you do while you are driving? How much attention do you give the people in your life? What is taking your free time? It might be time to de-clutter. It might be time to set some boundaries or limits. Maybe you need to find some safe, peaceful places or people that help you to stay grounded. Whatever it is you need to do in your life to be more present or more still, you will quickly find that the benefits far outweigh the sacrifices. Learning to be still in your life is a gift you are desperately in need of—you just don't know it.

Action Questions

- How can you create more "be still" time in your life?
- What can you do to disconnect from things that prevent you from living your life?
- In what ways can you be more present in your life and relationships?
- Do you have a place where you can recharge, listen, and seek peace? If not, find one.

TWELVE

The Weightier Matters

*Woe unto you, scribes and Pharisees, hypocrites! For ye pay tithe
of mint and anise and cummin, and have omitted the weightier
matters of the law, judgment, mercy, and faith; these ought ye to
have done, and not to leave the other undone.*

—MATTHEW 23:23

Years ago during a staff meeting, one of my coworkers was
sitting on the window sill while the rest of us were at the "round
table." Another coworker asked her why she was sitting there.
Her reply caught me off guard. "Today I feel kind of like a
wilting flower and I need to lean toward the sun," she said
with a smile. How often do we feel drained, stressed, lonely,
tired, beaten, or discouraged, kind of like a wilting flower? Yet
I wonder how often our answer is to lean toward the Son, the
Lord Jesus Christ.

I am terrible with plants and they have to be wilting or
dying before I notice and give them sunlight. Sometimes we
treat our souls the same way, waiting to reach for our true
Light, the Son of God, until we are wilting or dying. Flowers
are smart—they lean toward the sun. They are attracted to light.
In fact many types of plants lean toward the sun. Why then do

we, as humans, tend to avoid the Son at all costs? We seem less and less attracted by the Light and more and more attracted to darkness. We fill our lives with things such as "mint, anise and cummin" but forget the "weightier things." We get consumed and overwhelmed with work, play, family, etc., and sometimes forget to read our scriptures, do our visiting/home teaching, say our prayers, pay tithing, and go to the temple regularly. It seems we are always trying to fit our prayers and scripture studying into our busy day, instead of the other way around.

REMEMBER

When I was about fifteen, my grandpa taught a Sunday School lesson where he asked the class what the most important word was. The students came up with many important words, and my grandfather wrote them all over the chalkboard. Once we had exhausted our ideas, he took one of those long erasers and erased a space in the center of the chalkboard. Then he wrote the word *REMEMBER*. That lesson, and the image of the chalkboard with the word *remember* written in capital letters has stayed with me all these years. In fact, years ago when I was on a study-abroad trip in Jerusalem, everyone was getting his or her name in Hebrew put on rings or necklaces to take back to the States. I didn't want my name on my ring and tried to think of a word that would be meaningful to me. That Sunday School lesson came to my mind, and I decided to get the word *remember* (וכזל) put on my ring. When I look at the ring, I focus on remembering what really matters.

On my mission, I was asked to teach some missionaries at a meeting. I was told to choose my own topic, which was a bit overwhelming. As I was studying the missionary companionship of Alma and Amulek in the Book of Mormon, I noticed again the importance of the word *remember*. The Lord commands Alma and Amulek to teach the people in the city of Ammonihah. Notice the first thing Alma says to them.

> *And I stood with boldness to declare unto them, yea, I did boldly testify unto them, saying: Behold, O ye wicked and perverse generation, how have ye forgotten the tradition of your fathers; yea, how soon ye have forgotten the commandments of God. Do ye not* remember *that our father, Lehi, was brought out of Jerusalem by the hand of God? Do ye not* remember *that they were all led by him through the wilderness?. . .*
>
> *Behold, do ye not* remember *the words which he spake unto Lehi, saying that: Inasmuch as ye shall keep my commandments, ye shall prosper in the land? And again it is said that: Inasmuch as ye will not keep my commandments ye shall be cut off from the presence of the Lord. Now I would that ye should* remember, *that inasmuch as the Lamanites have not kept the commandments of God, they have been cut off from the presence of the Lord. (*Alma 9:8–9, 13–14; emphasis added)

Before he teaches the people about Christ, the Atonement, and repentance, Alma teaches them to remember their fathers and to remember God, who had delivered them. Every Sunday in the sacrament prayers, we hear the phrase "always remember him" (Doctrine and Covenants 20:77, 79). So I taught the missionaries that they needed to teach their investigators to remember, to read their scriptures so they could remember their fathers, and so that they could remember that God did and will deliver His people. Remembering opens our hearts and helps us to feel the Spirit. Once we have open hearts, we can begin to study our scriptures in a way that will transform our lives.

A SERIOUS STUDY

Ezra Taft Benson said, "There is a power in the [Book of Mormon] which will begin to flow into your life the moment you begin a serious study of the book" (Benson, "Gifts and Expectations," 1986, 7). Serious scripture study is one thing a lot of singles struggle with or completely omit from their lives. We all know we need to read our scriptures, but we come up with excuses not to do it on a regular basis. More often than I would like to admit, I have a love/hate relationship with my scriptures. When I read them consistently, I love them and they truly bless my life. The times in my life when I just can't find the time or even desire to read the scriptures, it becomes so easy to not read them, and mustering up the desire to do so seems like such a chore. Perhaps you can relate.

Sometimes in life we just have to pay the price. With the scriptures, we need to not just read them but study them. I have found in my life that when I approach the scriptures in a variety of ways, they come alive to me. I also find my study becomes much less casual. When I am truly studying, not just reading, you will find me on the floor with a notebook, my scriptures, my laptop (the Church has excellent resources on lds.org), some kind of reference book, colored pencils, and a pen. I am just digging into the scriptures and loving it. Here are a few of the different ways I like to study my scriptures.

Key Words or Phrases

2 Kings 6:15–17

> *And when the servant of the man of God was risen early, and gone forth, behold, an host compassed the city both with horses and chariots. And his servant said unto him, Alas, my master! how shall we do?*
>
> *And he answered, Fear not: for they that be with us are more than they that be with them.*
>
> *And Elisha prayed, and said, Lord, I pray thee, open his eyes, that he may see. And the Lord opened the eyes of the young man; and he saw: and, behold, the mountain was full of horses and chariots of fire round about Elisha.*

Esther 4:13–14

> *Then Mordecai commanded to answer Esther, Think not with thyself that thou shalt escape in the king's house, more than all the Jews.*

> *For if thou altogether holdest thy peace at this time,*
> *then shall there enlargement and deliverance arise to*
> *the Jews from another place; but thou and thy father's*
> *house shall be destroyed: and who knoweth whether*
> *thou art come to the kingdom for such a time as this?*

Both of these stories of faith contain key phrases that teach great truths. The verses from 2 Kings tell of a servant who couldn't see the chariots of the spirits that were there to fight the battle for God. The lesson is that each of us needs to open our spiritual eyes to see the workings of our Heavenly Father in our lives. 2 Kings 6:16 contains the powerful phrase "They that be with us are more than they that be with them." In every situation or trial we might encounter, we can rest assured that God will eventually prevail, for He is much stronger than Satan and his minions.

In the excerpt from the book of Esther, we learn of a young woman's remarkable faith. Esther chooses to save her people, the Jews, even as she risks her own life. Her story is empowering not only for women but for everyone who must stand for truth and righteousness in dire circumstances. A key phrase in the account is "Who knoweth whether thou art come to the kingdom for such a time as this?" (Esther 4:14). This question is a reminder that each of us has a specific purpose here on earth. There are things only you can do!

When teachers or students discuss the above passages, they usually speak only of the miracles of Moses parting the Red Sea and the Israelites crossing on dry land, or Peter walking on water before he loses faith and falters. The obvious, external meanings of these passages are powerful, but I think these verses can also teach us something entirely different.

In my own scriptures, I have highlighted two different principles in these passages—principles that are rarely discussed. The phrases I chose to study were "that they go forward" and "when Peter was come down out of the ship." These phrases teach us of the kind of faith and action that must happen before miracles can occur. The children of Israel needed to have the faith to walk into the Red Sea, just like Peter needed faith followed by action to step out of the boat into the water. As you can see, simply choosing to study different principles or phrases—sometimes those that may seem unimportant at first—can change a passage of scripture entirely.

Patterns or Themes

Mosiah 26:2—4

They did not *believe what had been said concerning the resurrection of the dead, neither did they believe concerning the coming of Christ.*

And now because of their unbelief they could not *understand the word of God; and their hearts were hardened.*

And they would not *be baptized; neither would they join the church. And they were a separate people as to their faith, and remained so ever after, even in their carnal and sinful state; for they* would not *call upon the Lord their God.* (emphasis added)

Sometimes patterns are not obvious at first, but once you start looking for them you will notice them everywhere in the scriptures. The above passage describes an all-too-familiar pattern—unbelief leading to not understanding and then ultimately to not receiving blessings. I wonder how many times in my life I have missed out on great growth, wonderful experiences, and enlightenment because of a "did not, could not, would not" attitude. I choose instead to be a Do-Can-Willer!

Cause and Effect

Doctrine and Covenants 130:20–21

> *There is a law, irrevocably decreed in heaven before the foundations of this word, upon which all blessings are predicated—*
>
> *And when we obtain any blessing from God, it is by obedience to that law upon which it is predicated.*

When looking for cause-and-effect relationships in the scriptures, you can start with the cause or start with the effect. In the above passage, we learn that when we obey certain laws we receive blessings. This principle, cause and effect, is woven throughout the scriptures.

Scripture Mastery and Cross References

Moses 1:18

> *And the Lord called His people Zion, because they were of one heart and one mind, and dwelt in righteousness; and there was no poor among them.*

Sometimes it helps to go back to the basics of seminary and re-memorize the scripture-mastery scriptures. Take it to another level by following the cross-references and reading those scriptures to help you to better understand the passage you are studying.

Topical Study

Fear

Exodus 14:13	"Fear ye not, stand still and see the salvation of the Lord."
Matthew 14:27	"Be of good cheer: it is I: be not afraid."
Moroni 8:16	"Perfect love casteth out all fear."
Doctrine and Covenants 6:30	"Look unto me in every thought; doubt not, fear not"
Doctrine and Covenants 50:41	"Fear not, little children, for you are mine."
2 Kings 6:16	"Fear not: for they that be with us are more than they that be with them."

Proverbs 29:25	"The fear of man bringeth a snare: but whoso putteth his trust in the Lord shall be safe."
Isaiah 51:7	"Fear ye not the reproach of men."
Luke 12:32	"Fear not, little flock."
2 Timothy 1:7	"God hath not given us the spirit of fear."

When studying the scriptures by topic, it is easy to look it up in the topical guide and read the scriptural references. However, the real challenge—the fun part—is to start making *other* connections between the related passages. For instance, using the topic above, fear, we can see a principle emerge—that with God we don't need to fear. He will fight for us and call us His own. As you study the scriptures by topic, you begin to understand that topic more in depth and also to appreciate the many layers the different books of scriptures bring to it.

Other Ideas

One idea for studying your scriptures is to use a color code for marking certain words or topics. This will help you to easily locate those topics and words. Another way to study is by creating scripture chains, where you find one scripture then follow a cross-reference to the next scripture, and so forth. A fun idea is to pose a question and use your study time to answer that question with as many scriptures as possible. Another way is to set a certain amount of time to read. Of course you can combine many of these methods in your study.

Studying the scriptures is very personal and unique to each individual. The list of techniques I have offered here is not comprehensive. I encourage you to find your own ways to study the scriptures. If you are struggling to read the scriptures on a regular basis, ask someone to hold you accountable by regularly asking you about your reading.

PRINCIPLES OF PRAYER

Another "weightier matter" many people struggle with is personal prayer. As I talk with friends, they sometimes express frustration with the inconsistency of their prayers. Some friends say they have a hard time feeling the Spirit in their lives, including when they pray. They ask me, "Why would I pray when my prayers aren't getting answered and I don't feel the Spirit?" Having been there myself, I completely understand this reasoning. However, we all know that distancing ourselves from God is not the way to find answers or peace in our lives.

Before I share with you a principle of prayer I discovered in the scriptures, I need to give one caveat. The Lord will *always* listen to your prayers. If you are about to crash into another car and scream out a pleading prayer, if you are not in a place where you can kneel but need to talk with the Lord, if you are in utter despair or stress and can't even communicate clearly—no matter the situation, the Lord will hear your prayer. The process below is for the regular daily prayers we offer. As you know, you get more out of something when you put more in, and that holds true for prayer.

Years ago, I was asked to give a sacrament-meeting talk about prayer. Before I studied for that talk, I don't think I gave prayer much thought. I grew up in a home where we prayed often, so I was taught to pray when I was very little, and praying came natural to me. Therefore, when I was asked to give a talk about prayer, I had no idea what I would say. As I studied the scriptures, I was enlightened as to the process of prayer. Here are some of things I learned.

THE PROCESS OF PRAYER

SCRIPTURES	PRINCIPLES
James 4:3	Don't ask amiss.
Helaman 10:5	Don't ask contrary to God's will.
Doctrine and Covenants 46:30	Ask in the name of Jesus Christ.
Doctrine and Covenants 50:29–30	Be clean and purified. Be careful what you ask for.
3 Nephi 19:24	Listen to the Spirit.
Doctrine and Covenants 9:8–9	Study it out and then ask.
Ephesians 6:18	Pray "in the Spirit."
2 Chronicles 7:14	Humble yourself, seek His face, and turn from wickedness.

"Prayer" in Topical Guide (752–53)	Prayer is a form of work. "The object of prayer is not to change the will of God but to secure . . . blessings that God is already willing to grant . . . conditional on our asking for them."

As you read through these scriptures, you will find that the process of prayer isn't simply to kneel down, fold your arms, and start talking. The scriptures teach us that there are many principles involved in prayer. The environment we pray in, our spiritual and physical state, what we ask for, how we ask, and our willingness to listen are all key elements in the process of prayer.

You can apply all of the other principles in this book, but if you don't apply the principles in this chapter you will come up short. There is a reason we have what we refer to as "Sunday School answers." Basic principles are the foundation upon which all other principles are built. When you gain a testimony of the power of prayer, scripture study, keeping the commandments, going to the temple, and so forth, you can add other principles, line upon line. When these "weightier matters" are overlooked or neglected, it is hard to maintain other areas of your life. Digging into the scriptures, calling upon Heavenly Father, and building a relationship with Jesus Christ will help you discover what you need in your life to be happy.

Action Questions

- What things do you need to prioritize in your life?
- Can you think of other ways to study your scriptures?
- How do you dig into your scriptures and apply them to your life?
- In what ways can you place greater emphasis on the "weightier matters"?

THIRTEEN
Building the Kingdom

*Men and women who turn their lives over to God will discover
that He can make a lot more out of their lives than they can.
He will deepen their joys, expand their vision, quicken
their minds, strengthen their muscles, lift their spirits, multiply
their blessings, increase their opportunities, comfort their souls,
raise up friends, and pour out peace.*
—EZRA TAFT BENSON ("JESUS CHRIST," 1998)

I think many singles in the Church have gotten lazy when it comes to building the kingdom. When people get married and have kids, they wear out their lives in service of each other and their children. They do this while keeping jobs, fulfilling Church callings, and a myriad of other things. When someone is single, he or she has the same responsibility to build the kingdom and to serve, but without a spouse and children, the person might think he or she is off the hook. This is just not the case. I believe singles have the same responsibility as any married person, mother, or father, to use their talents and time to build the kingdom of God. Being single is not an excuse to be selfish.

If you are anxiously engaged in doing God's work, you can no longer use the excuse that you don't fit, that this church is only for families, or whatever excuse you use to feel out of place or like a misfit. While serving in the Relief Society general presidency, Chieko Okazaki said:

Reasons to stay: the value of diversity: If you experience the pain of exclusion at church from someone who is frightened at your difference, please don't leave [or] become inactive. You may think you are voting with your feet, that you are making a statement by leaving. [Some may] see your diversity as a problem to be fixed, as a flaw to be corrected or erased. If you are gone, they don't have to deal with you anymore. I want you to know that your diversity is a more valuable statement. (Okazaki, *Cat's Cradle,* 1993)

When we aren't building the kingdom, feelings of inadequacy can creep in and choke our ability to be happy. So what does it mean to build the kingdom? Basically, it boils down to the threefold mission of the Church: perfecting the saints, redeeming the dead, and proclaiming the gospel. It's being a Christian in every aspect of your life. It is using your time, talents, and energy to help create Zion. No doubt you are aware of which people in your life are actively building the kingdom—and which ones are not. Henry Emerson Fosdick wrote:

Some Christians carry their religion on their backs. It is a packet of beliefs and practices which they must bear. At times it grows heavy and they would willingly lay it down, but that would mean a break in old traditions, so they shoulder it again. But real Christians do not carry their religion, their religion carries them. It is not weight; it is wings. It lifts them up, it sees them over hard places, it makes the universe seem friendly, life purposeful, hope real, sacrifice worthwhile. It sets them free from fear, futility, discouragement, and sin— the great enslavers of men's souls. You can know a real Christian when you see him, by his buoyancy. (Fosdick, *Twelve Tests of Character,* 1923, 87–88)

You truly can see the difference between those who build the kingdom and allow the doctrine to fill their souls and give them wings, and those who feel shackled.

Here are some principles that have helped me to dig in and build the kingdom wherever I am.

UNPACK YOUR SUITCASE

When I first arrived in the mission field, my mission president told all of the new missionaries to unpack our suitcases immediately. He said missionaries often live out of their suitcases because they never know when they are going to be transferred and it's easier that way. He told us to never do that. We needed to unpack our suitcases, hang up our clothes or put them in drawers, and find a place for our toothbrushes. He wanted us to understand the idea of firmly planting ourselves in the area in which we were serving.

This had a powerful effect on me on my mission, but even more of an effect on my life *after* my mission. Let me explain. I have a very strong case of wanderlust and therefore find myself moving every few years. As a result I have lived in many different places, had several different jobs, and met a lot of amazing people. Whenever I move to a new place I remember what I learned from my mission and I unpack my suitcase. I plant my feet where I am and I dig in. I try not to compare where I am to where I have been or where I hope to go. By doing this, I have been able to make long-lasting friendships and priceless connections. I think this same principle can be applied toward building the kingdom.

When I decided to go to grad school, I chose Arizona State University (ASU), but I wasn't too enthusiastic to move to Mesa, Arizona. In fact, although I knew ASU was the right school for me (this decision did not come easily), I didn't feel Arizona was the right place for me to live. When I got there, I thought the thermometer must be broken in my car because it said it was 116 degrees outside. I called my parents to let them know I'd arrived in Egypt. I was overwhelmed with anticipation for grad school, moving to a new state, and meeting my new roommates. Soon I had to decide what I wanted to do about church. I could either go to the singles ward in Mesa or attend my university ward in Tempe. Deciding to attend my university ward, the University 5th Ward, significantly impacted my life for the next two years.

The first time I went to the U5 Ward, it was testimony meeting. The first three people to share their testimonies were young men who were announcing their mission calls or leaving for their missions. I couldn't believe how young my new ward was. I was twenty-eight and the oldest person in the ward by a long shot, aside from the bishopric. I sat there thinking I had made a mistake. Somehow I had arrived in Egypt, was now attending the youngest singles ward in the world, and I didn't know a soul. Almost on auto pilot I began to unpack my suitcases literally and figuratively. I told myself I wouldn't complain about Arizona for at least six months, that I wouldn't compare Mesa to Boston, and that if I could survive the freezing tundra of Massachusetts in the winter, I could endure the burning inferno of Arizona's summer.

I grew to love my young university ward. I met some amazing people and made some incredible friends. But most importantly, I began to understand that the Lord will use me wherever I am. When I am willing to show Him I am ready to be an instrument in His hands, it doesn't matter if I am the oldest person in the singles ward or just graduated from high school and am going to a singles ward for the first time. Unpacking your suitcase and settling into your life, wherever you may be, will not only bless your life but will help you to magnify your gifts and talents in building the kingdom of God.

MAGNIFY YOUR CORNER

I received a letter from Janice Kapp Perry while on my mission. She had been given my CD of original songs and was writing to let me know she had received it and was passing it on to someone else, since she was leaving for her own mission. She described her history of writing music and how she was commissioned to write music for the Church. She said she didn't start writing music until her kids were mostly grown and out of the house. Then she started writing for the young women in her ward, and from there was asked to write for the youth in her stake. Eventually she was commissioned to write for the youth of the Church. Sister Perry told me it was never her intention to be a famous musician. She just loved music, and she loved the youth of the Church. As a result, the Lord magnified her little corner of the world, and she was able to bless more lives than she could ever imagine. She challenged me as a missionary and as a musician to magnify my corner and not to worry about anything else. If I magnified my little corner, she said, the Lord would do the rest. If I did my best to teach the people in my area, at the visitor's center, and at the temple, the Lord would take care of the rest. I have thought often about Sister Perry's advice and tried to apply it in building the kingdom.

What do you have that makes you unique? What gifts or talents do you possess that you can share to build the kingdom? Can you be a better visiting teacher or home teacher? Can you serve better in your calling? Can you be a better employee or employer? What do you need to do in your life to magnify your corner?

LIVE BY FAITH

I have heard many single adults in the Church ask why they are single. They don't understand why their plan and Heavenly Father's plan seem to be different. They are often desperate to understand His will in order to figure out what to do with their lives. I know this feeling well. It is almost as if they are saying that living their faith-filled lives isn't enough. They want to understand Heavenly Father's will and to feel that He hears them and knows them. I have spent a fair amount of time seeking out my purpose in life. It seems that as soon as I figure out what to do, things change. I feel as if the Lord is closing doors in my life and I'm struggling to open them and run through before He shuts the next door. He is trying to communicate to me to be still and live by faith, and I'm trying to make things happen. And then without fireworks or a burning in the bosom, I hear the Spirit whisper to my soul. I take a deep breath and relearn what it means to have faith.

Faith is power, faith is work, faith is a choice, and faith is fueled by belief. Faith can raise the dead, heal the sick, bring sight to the blind, and change your heart. Faith can also help you find your keys, bear your testimony, approach that person you have been meaning to talk to for a while, and strengthen your relationships with others. Living by faith means believing in miracles, and trusting that God knows best.

Elder Gene R. Cook of the Quorum of the Seventy said:

Today is a day of miracles. We believe in miracles. The Latter-day Saints may expect miracles according to their faith. As a member of this Church, you are authorized to take a leading part in the development of the kingdom of God on earth within your respective responsibilities. Pray fervently. Actively seek to increase your faith, and with that great gift from God, you can cause great things to occur. (Cook, "Faith in the Lord," 1981)

I believe in miracles and that faith can move mountains, shut lions' mouths, deliver prophets from fires, save a missionary from the belly of a whale, turn a rod into a snake, and rain manna from heaven. But I also believe in quiet lives filled with faith, people who magnify their callings and breathe the love of God into everyone they come into contact with. I stand in awe at the Prophet Joseph Smith and his brother Hyrum, who suffered so much for the kingdom of God and even gave their lives for it. With the same esteem, I reverence women who hold Primary callings for longer than I have been alive, men who never get to sit with their families in sacrament meeting because they are always on the stand, and the faithful elderly man who greets everyone at the chapel doors with a welcome smile and candy in his coat pocket. These faithful men and women understand what it means to live by faith. Their lives pay tribute to God and proclaim salvation to everyone they meet.

As you live by faith, people will notice. Your faith-filled life will radiate not only God's love but the happiness you feel. Without saying a word, your life as a disciple of Christ will testify to everyone around you. But this isn't enough. The world is filled with people who are desperate to find truth. They are searching for God and straining to hear His voice. They may notice the light you carry, but they will probably need you to invite them to the truth.

EVERY MEMBER A MISSIONARY

A big part of building the kingdom is being a missionary, and being single does not give you an exemption. Having served a full-time mission doesn't get you off the hook, either. I know that because I served a mission I should be happy sharing the gospel, or at least be good at it, but most of the time, I'm neither.

I don't mind living the gospel, talking about the Church, and even inviting friends to Church activities, but when it comes to being a member missionary I come up short. It is always hard to take something you love and willingly share it with others. There's always the worry that they may hate it, reject it, criticize it, and so forth. But—and this is the best part—they may love it and accept it, and it may change their lives dramatically. Our job isn't to make the choice for them. Our job is to share the gospel willingly and freely and leave the rest to the Lord! So why is it that our part seems so hard?

On my mission, there was a point where I stopped feeling that I was bugging people when I told them about the gospel, and started feeling that they needed to hear the gospel because it would change their lives. I found myself shouting the gospel from the rooftops—well, not exactly, but I didn't want to miss an opportunity to teach anyone. When I got home from my mission, I slipped back into how I had felt as a green missionary. I felt I was bothering people by sharing the gospel with them. I figured they would just say no, so why bother? But I had some experiences in Boston a few years ago that helped me realize that sharing the gospel can be fun, natural, and enjoyable.

IF YOU LOVE IT, SHARE IT

I love to drink water, and my favorite kind of flavored water is Lemon Propel. A few years ago, on a walking lunch with a coworker, I introduced her to Lemon Propel. It was an instant hit, so much so that I fear she may be addicted. Once she tried Lemon Propel, she told everyone else in the office and all her friends about it. At one point, if you were to look up at our office from the ground, you'd see one windowsill lined with empty Lemon Propel bottles, and you might think we were getting paid to advertise.

When blogging was brand new and you had to write your own HTML, I started blogging and instantly loved it. I had to tell everyone about it. The point is that when you love something you just want to share it with everyone you know. Of course, this is also true when it comes to the gospel.

One day on my way to work in Boston, I got onto the subway. I usually love getting on the T—watching people, trying to write their stories in my mind—but that day I was oblivious to everyone else. I was running late, the bus took forever getting me to the T, and I was behind at work because I didn't go in the day before due to illness. As I was getting situated in my seat on the T, I had my headphones on, but this little old lady tapped me on my shoulder and asked if I was Mormon. I took off my headphones and stared at her, thinking I'd heard her wrong. She repeated, "Are you Mormon? I saw your book in your bag." I was startled and pulled out my military copy of the Book of Mormon. "Oh, this." I nodded in her direction. "Oh, yes," she said, "I've had some young gentlemen try to convert me with that book before." At this point I realized we were going to discuss the gospel right there on the T, and I wasn't ready.

Naturally, I asked her, "So what did you think?" She smiled up at me, chuckled, and said, "They did a good job trying to convert me." There was that awful word—*convert*—again, and it was said in such a negative tone. She turned away, but after a few minutes of trying to read, I tapped her on the shoulder. "Ma'am, were they kind, the young men?" She smiled at me again and said, "Well, yes, dear. In fact, I have been visited by a few of them since my first visit." I said, "You can't blame them, can you?" She looked puzzled and asked, "Blame them for what?" That was exactly the reaction I wanted. I said, "You can't blame them for wanting to share something they love." She laughed out loud and her laugh seemed to dissolve any awkwardness between us. I talked to her about serving a mission myself (she was surprised that women serve missions), and for a few brief moments our hearts connected. Sharing the gospel never felt so natural and easy.

Fast-forward a few years. Several months ago, I had a missionary experience. One of my coworkers doesn't know much about Mormons, so we'd talked a little bit about the Church and I had invited him to check out lds.org. One day at work he told me that he has been seeing those "kids with the white shirts and ties and bikes" around his neighborhood a lot. I laughed. He asked me what they were doing there. I told him, "They are looking for you." He laughed and asked why. I told him the truth—"Because I have been praying them into your life." He teased me a bit, but then we had a great conversation about missionaries. I told him about my own Church mission, and he asked a lot of questions. I bore my testimony right there at work; it didn't even freak him out.

As we focus our lives on Christ and building the kingdom, He will do amazing things with us and for us. From personal experience and from watching other people, I have learned that we become successful and happy only when we put God first. If you want to fit into the Church, if you want to be a part of something incredible, if you want to use your talents to the utmost, you need to build the kingdom. When you make a concerted effort to do so, other things in your life will fall into place.

Action Questions

- How do you carry your Christianity—is it a weight or wings in your life?
- In what ways can you "unpack your suitcase" in your life? How can you live in the present and not in comparisons?
- How can you magnify your corner of the world?
- How can you infuse more faith into yourself and into your life?
- What are you doing in your single life to build the kingdom?

FOURTEEN

The Other Great Commandment

We receive mixed messages today that self-love and a sense of self-worth are forms of selfishness and conceit. However, I know from my own experience that when I don't fully accept myself and all of my warts, blemishes, and imperfections, I am crippled in my charity toward God and my neighbors. Let me encourage you not to feel guilty as you aspire to appropriate self-love, which comes in part by honest self-knowledge and acceptance.

—JEFFREY R. AND PATRICIA T. HOLLAND, *ON EARTH AS IT IS IN HEAVEN*, 1989.

We've all heard a flight attendant tell passengers to put on their oxygen masks before trying to help anyone else. It makes sense that you need to be able to breathe in order to assist another person, but there's a reason they tell you this every time you get on a plane. When you love someone, you naturally want to protect him or her first. In times of emergency, a parent will want to help a child before helping himself or herself. On an airplane when cabin pressure is lost, this is problematic. If a child can breathe because she is wearing her mask but the parent passes out because he didn't put his mask on first, he obviously can't help the child if there are further problems.

In the New Testament, Jesus Christ explains a similar principle. I like to call it the "other" great commandment.

Then one of them, which was a lawyer, asked him a question, tempting him, and saying,

Master, which is the great commandment in the law?

Jesus said unto him, Thou shalt love the Lord thy God with all thy heart, and with all thy soul, and with all thy mind.

This is the first and great commandment.

And the second is like unto it, Thou shalt love thy neighbor as thyself. (Matthew 22:35–39)

Notice there are two parts to the second great commandment. The first part is to love yourself, and the second is to love your neighbor. For the sake of this chapter I want to focus on the first part of the second great commandment: to love yourself.

Many times in the scriptures, the Lord teaches the principle of taking care of oneself before serving or teaching others. For example, we read in Luke 22:32, "When thou are converted, strengthen thy brethren." Here the Lord is teaching Peter that before he can convert others to the gospel, he must first be converted. Another instance is found in a revelation the Prophet Joseph Smith received for his brother Hyrum. In it, the Lord counsels Hyrum, "Seek not to declare my word, but first seek to obtain my word" (Doctrine and Covenants 11:21). In both of these examples, the Lord explains that if we want to teach others, serve others, or strengthen others, first we have to take care of ourselves.

You may be thinking it seems prideful to think of yourself first. You may also feel you don't have time in your life to set aside just for yourself. As someone who has been single for a long time, I get that. Often, I fill up my schedule with so many things that I don't have time to feel lonely. But I'm sure you understand the idea of good, better, and best. The Lord has counseled us not to run faster than we have strength, and that milk comes before meat. No doubt you understand what it means to be anxiously engaged, build the kingdom, and be an instrument in the Lord's hand. We all try to do good when and where we can. Where I think some of us get lost is in *implementing* these critical principles. How do we do all the above while still finding time for ourselves? And even more importantly, how do we love others when we don't love ourselves?

LOVE THYSELF

As a ten-year-old, I was handing out my school pictures to my aunts, uncles, and my grandma. I was pretty proud of my picture, and as I handed one to my grandma, I said, "Aren't I darling?" Instead of agreeing with me, my grandma told me I shouldn't brag about myself like that. After that, my fearless inhibitions and love of myself started getting buried by how the world taught me to think about myself. I started caring more about what others thought about me than what God thought of me or what I thought of myself.

I see this all the time in people. They are so busy trying to make others happy or feel loved that they have lost their sense of self-love. One time while teaching a Relief Society lesson, I asked the sisters how many of them knew that God and Jesus Christ loved them. I was astonished at how few sisters raised their hands. How do you give what you don't have? How do you do your home or visiting teaching and truly love your teachees if you don't love yourself? I think somehow in trying to please everyone, trying to be the person others expect us to be, we've forgotten who we are. We have forgotten that "The Lord seeth not as man seeth; for man looketh on the outward appearance, but the Lord looketh on the heart" (1 Samuel 16:7). We would do ourselves a big favor if we could rediscover a bit of our ten-year-old selves.

At times, we focus on the person or people in our lives who have the greatest influence over us and lose focus on the person who matters the most. God is waiting for us to remember who we are, where we came from, and our purpose here on earth. He is ready to show us how much He loves us if we will only ask Him. Relearning how to love yourself isn't an easy task, and it takes time. Here are a few ways to get started.

NEGOTIABLE SPACE

Most of us look at our schedules, at our lives, and think, "Okay, here are all the things I need to do. These are all the ways I need to serve others. These are all the ways I need to be obedient and serve God." We start making a list and filling our schedule with good and great things. We start trying to serve people all over the place. We do a lot of good and better things but end up feeling a little empty. Sure, you are staying busy, furthering your education, climbing the ladder of success at your job, dating, socializing, and doing your home teaching or visiting teaching. But sometimes when the day is done you're still left feeling incomplete, lonely, and wondering why you aren't happy.

In all the craziness that is your life, in all your efforts to be anxiously engaged in doing good, perhaps you are simply forgetting yourself. Maybe you forget the things that make you happy, and you stop doing the little things that make you smile. Somewhere along the road, you probably decided that everyone and everything else comes first and that your personal time is whatever is left. At general conference in October 2010, President Dieter F. Uchtdorf declared:

> *Let's be honest; it's rather easy to be busy. We all can think up a list of tasks that will overwhelm our schedules. Some might even think that their self-worth depends on the length of their to-do list. They flood the open spaces in their time with lists of meetings and minutia—even during times of stress and fatigue. Because they unnecessarily complicate their lives, they often feel increased frustration, diminished joy, and too little sense of meaning in their lives.* (Uchtdorf, "Matter Most," 2010)

Don't get me wrong—living a full life is great, but as I mentioned earlier, cramming our schedules to the brim isn't the best way to live. I think there is another way to apply the above-mentioned principles. Instead of filling up all my free time in a given week, I leave some large blocks of time, and some small ones, where I don't plan anything at all. This is what I call negotiable space. When I first did this I felt a bit uncomfortable, almost selfish, to have downtime. Then something magical happened—the Lord took that space and used it for His purposes. He brought people to me, people I needed to serve. In addition, I had time to do things for myself, like reading books I had been meaning to read, going running, playing the piano just for fun, and writing poetry, letters, and blog entries, as well as writing in my journal. He helped me realize I desperately needed to strengthen myself before I could be of use to anyone else.

If you start leaving free blocks of time in your schedule, you will soon find you are just as busy as you were before, but you will feel much different. You will have learned to love yourself, and you will use your time in the best possible ways. You will come to realize that God can do so much more with your time than you ever could. When this happens you are ready to fulfill the second part of the second great commandment.

BE INSPIRED SO YOU CAN INSPIRE

As I speak to singles, a major theme tends to emerge. At some point along the way, single people get stuck. Sometimes it's after a mission, after graduation, after grad school, or after a breakup. In these moments, we can get frustrated, and we tend to lack the motivation or inspiration to figure out what to do next. For most of us, this is when we look to others to figure out what is wrong with us or tell us what to do with our lives.

Often, we pray and ask God to tell us what to do and when He doesn't lay out our path, we get frustrated. We expect others to enlighten us or inspire us, and we are let down time and time again. Over the years I have learned there's a better way.

If you are in need of motivation or direction, it's time for you to seek inspiration. To begin you might need to find some physical places that inspire you. Maybe it's the corner of a certain restaurant, an art studio, your home library, your kitchen, the back-porch swing, or the old bookstore downtown. Being in a place that feels like "home" can help you begin your journey of inspiration.

In almost every class in my social-work grad-school program, we were asked what we do for self-care. When you are dealing with other people's trauma, it is important to take care of yourself. I'll never forget the first time I was called to share my self-care plan. I stood and told my classmates that I like to spend time on swings. They all started laughing, and my teacher told me that was a first for her. She asked me why I like to swing. I told her I've lived in many different places and that the first thing I do when I move to a new city is find a swing set that is near my house. That way, no matter what is going on in my life, I always know where to go to find peace and inspiration. Sometimes I go to swing just for the ambience, and sometimes I go and pour my heart out to God. Where there are swings, there are usually kids, parents, couples walking, people interacting with each other, and a lot of joy. No matter how my day has gone or how bad I'm feeling, I can't help but be uplifted. I find myself lost in the motion of the swing, in the memories of when I was kid and would spend time on the swings with my friends and siblings. I find myself looking up in the sky, freeing my mind of negative thoughts and feelings, and being inspired.

Another good thing is to surround yourself with people who inspire you to be better, to explore your options, and to keep stretching. Such people can be a profound influence in your life. Be wise in selecting those you go to when you are searching for answers or direction in your life. Also, know that it's okay to take time away from people who are negative, people who take all your energy and don't replace it with something inspiring, and people who stifle inspiration. Seek out people who open your eyes to new ideas, exciting experiences, new places, new hobbies, new passion, and new friendship.

When I was a junior in high school, a new girl named Nicole started attending our cooking class. She brought a woman with her, but most of the time the woman just sat silently at the table next to Nicole. One day when the teacher was explaining something, he turned around to do something with the stove but continued to talk. All of a sudden the woman next to Nicole started moving her hands in these beautiful expressions, and I realized Nicole was deaf. I couldn't believe it because she could talk, and it seemed as if she could hear because she didn't miss a beat. She had gone to a special school for years to learn how to lip-read and speak, but she was ready to attend a regular high school. Nicole only needed her interpreter when the teacher wasn't facing the students. I had no idea the inspiration Nicole and her interpreter would play in my life. Because a few of my cooking classmates and I were intrigued by American Sign Language (ASL), Nicole and her interpreter taught us some ASL after school. I enjoyed learning sign language, so I took it as my language in college, served an ASL mission, and have been blessed to have many amazing experiences with the language.

Lastly, seek inspiration in the things you already have a passion for or talents you have already developed. I've noticed that our passions, hobbies, and talents are usually the first things to go when we are stressed, busy, or just trying to figure out our lives. When we leave these things out, we miss out on the inspiration they can bring.

TREAT YOURSELF WITH RESPECT

A big part of loving yourself is treating yourself with respect. I worked at a lockdown residential treatment center for adolescents. Many of the kids came to us because they were cutting themselves or using drugs. Many came to us from jail, from another treatment center, or from guardians who could no longer handle them. No matter the circumstances, all these adolescents came to us with little to no self-love or self-respect. Usually, this seems to be due to a lack of example and to the powerful influence of the world. The world is screaming that sex, drugs, flashy clothes, expensive cars, and having a perfect body will make you happy. My students struggled to simply feel loved by someone and couldn't even begin to love themselves.

One day I went to one of our girls' dorms and sat in a circle with the girls. I asked each girl to say something positive about the others in the circle, then something positive about herself, and then something positive about her body. None of the girls had a problem complimenting the other girls, but each one struggled tremendously to find something good about herself and her body. My heart broke for them.

In a world where it is "cool" to degrade yourself and your body, where advertisements and movies and TV speak far louder than the compliments of your peers, it is imperative to have a strong sense of self. Wouldn't it be great if we could surround ourselves with people who would constantly tell us how great and how beautiful or handsome we are? I wouldn't mind more validation in my life, but this just isn't realistic. There will be countless times in our lives when we will have to believe in and love ourselves no matter what anyone else says or does.

At the wilderness treatment center where I currently work, the focus is "Every child has a seed of greatness" (Ezekiel Sanchez). The idea is to build the confidence and self-esteem of each adolescent or adult that comes through the program. They do hard things, such as building fires, hiking all day, building shelters, and wading through rivers. As they do these things, they gain self-confidence and self-love. In addition, they are frequently reminded of their "seeds of greatness"— the good things about them. The change of heart that happens in these young people is remarkable. They learn to be happy and love themselves despite not being allowed to have any of their personal possessions and living in the wilderness for six weeks.

To love yourself and to love your body is so rare these days! My friends complain about their bodies all the time. They aren't thin enough, strong enough, tall enough, buff enough, or tan enough, and their hair isn't straight enough or curly enough.

They seem so concerned with how other people will view them and much less concerned about how they see themselves. Whenever I am in a group of singles, I see a lack of self-esteem and confidence. Most of us are attracted to those who exude confidence in who they are. You can usually feel when a person is content with who he or she is rather than trying to be someone else.

It is rare when someone is willing to share, in a raw and humble state, how she really feels about herself. My sister wrote a beautiful article where she talks about her body. I love her perspective. She writes:

I am enamored with my body. Proud. Grateful. Content. It might have something to do with the fact that I have spent the last two years of my life being sick. I lived on another continent and fought through four bouts of malaria, two cases of typhoid fever, ear infections, esophagitis, and more Montezuma's revenge than is appropriate to share. I got home, got healthy, got pregnant, and then went through nine months of continual morning sickness. I vomited day and night, with pills or without, no matter what I ate or what I did. I was miserable and depressed. I wanted my mind and my body back. The culmination of these physically difficult years was giving birth. It was traumatic and extraordinary at the same time. My body is far from "perfect," but I adore it. I am grateful every single day for it. I see my daughter's little pot belly arching over her diaper and smile, looking down at my little pouch, still loose and round. I know I should be ashamed of it, hide it, talk disparagingly about it, but right now the only word I can think of is "cute." Cute like her little belly. We match. (Chelsea Shields Strayer, "See the Temple," 2011)

I like how she knew she could be ashamed or hide her post-pregnancy belly but instead she loved herself. That belly represented her labor of love. I wish we could all be a little kinder to ourselves. Sure, most of us could afford to lose a little weight, spend more time at the gym, eat less (or at least eat healthier), but in the end no matter how we look, we should love who we are.

Make time in your life to take care of yourself. Create a self-care plan, one in which you take time to do things that bring you joy and peace. Carve out negotiable time in your life so the Lord can help you use that time for His purposes. Learn how to love yourself. In doing so, you will learn how to better love others.

Action Questions

- Make a list of ten qualities you love about yourself. Take time to rediscover what you are passionate about and what makes you tick.
- Where in your schedule can you free up some "negotiable space"?
- Who are the people that inspire you? Where are the places that make you feel free, safe, and creative? What can you do to inspire others?

- What things do you want to include in your self-care plan?
- How can you better learn to appreciate and love your body and your uniqueness?

FIFTEEN
Live the Questions

*Be patient with all that is unsolved in your heart and try to love
the questions themselves as if they were locked rooms or books
written in a foreign language. Do not now seek the answers,
which cannot be given you because you would not be able to live
them. And the point is, to live everything. Live the questions now.
Perhaps you will then gradually, without noticing it, live along
some distant day into the answer.*
—RAINER MARIE RILKE *(LETTERS,* 1934)

Though we live in a culture that caters to couples and families,
single people tend to go through the typical stages of life—
graduating from college, getting a job, starting a career, buying a
home, and so forth. We want to be happy and productive singles
but also want to get married and start a family, and therefore we
face unique challenges and sometimes ask difficult questions.

As I have passed through many different stages of life being
single, I have not only struggled with my own questions but
have coached those who love me and want happiness for me.
I have coached my parents through what it is like to be twenty-
five and single, twenty-eight and single, and now thirty-two and
single. The stages change but the questions are pretty much the

same: Why can't I find someone? Why don't I get to have kids? You know the questions—you've asked them a million times yourself. I've been able to do so much as a single person that I could never have done if I were married. At the same time I would love to be a mother. And I wish with all my heart that I could wrap up this book with the answers you are longing for. The truth is, there is no miraculous answer, but keep reading.

BELIEVE

In order to be happy in your present circumstances, you must believe. Believe you are meant to be happy in this life and the life to come. Believe God has a perfect plan for you. Believe you matter to those who know you. Believe you have a specific purpose and that you can live up to your potential. Believe you are loved—and act accordingly. Believe, and if for some reason you cannot, then borrow my belief in you for a few moments.

In the New Testament, we read of a father who brings his son to Jesus and asks Him to heal the young man, who has a "dumb spirit." The father tells Christ about the evil spirit that possesses his son. "Wheresoever he taketh him he teareth him: and he foameth and gnasheth with his teeth . . . and ofttimes it hast cast him into the fire, and into the waters, to destroy him: but if thou canst do anything, have compassion on us, and help us" (Mark 9:18, 22). I can picture this distraught father begging the Lord to heal his son. Jesus responds, "If thou canst believe, all things are possible to him that believeth" (v. 23). Then the miracle happens—"And straightway the father of the child cried out, and said with tears, Lord, I believe; help thou mine unbelief" (v. 24). I love this father for his humility, his faith, and his honesty. Just before he spoke to Christ, this man had already asked the disciples to heal his son and cast out the evil spirit, but they could not. In tears, he says he believes Christ can heal his son but that he needs help turning his belief into faith.

I can see myself in that father. I know how it feels to believe in something passionately and intellectually but lack the faith to turn that belief into action. In my opinion, pain and sorrow sometimes get in the way of developing true faith. Unfulfilled expectations of marriage, children, a home, and other dreams can make believing almost painful. It is hard to believe and hope when what you want the most doesn't happen and seems completely beyond your control. It is almost as if belief has a time limit—"I will believe for this amount of time, but after that I have to let go of my belief because it hurts too much." But the difference between believing and having faith is action.

Another scriptural lesson about belief and faith in the story of Jairus's daughter, as recorded in the New Testament. In Mark 5:23, Jairus, a ruler of the synagogue, pleads with Jesus to heal his daughter. "And besought Him greatly, saying, My little daughter lieth at the point of death: I pray thee, come and lay thy hands on her, that she may be healed; and she shall live." We learn in Luke's account that Jairus "had one only daughter, about twelve years of age" (Luke 8:42). Jesus follows Jairus, and as they are walking, they are approached by a servant from the house of Jairus. The servant says, "Thy daughter is dead: why troublest thou the Master any further?" (Mark 5:35). Jesus replies, "Be not afraid, only believe" (v. 36). At this point, He has quite a following of people, so He asks only Peter, James, and John to accompany Him to the home of Jairus. Mark 5: 38–40 reads:

And he cometh to the house of the ruler of the synagogue, and seeth the tumult, and them that wept and wailed greatly.

And when he was come in, he saith unto them, Why make ye this ado, and weep? the damsel is not dead, but sleepeth.

And they laughed him to scorn. But when he had put them all out, he taketh the father and the mother of the damsel, and them that were with him, and entereth in where the damsel was lying.

Then, those who believed and possessed faith were allowed to witness the miracle of Jesus raising Jairus's daughter from the dead (see vv. 41–42).

Several lessons about belief and faith are taught in this passage of scripture. First, I love Jairus's solid faith. When his servant tells Jairus that his daughter is dead, Jairus still has faith in Jesus. I want to exemplify that kind of belief in my life. Second, in one brief sentence, Jesus teaches that fear and faith cannot coexist. He says, "Be not afraid, only believe" (v. 36). Third, Jesus understands the importance of priesthood blessings, the environment in which they are to be administered, and the role of belief and faith in receiving the promises of a priesthood blessing. He invites only those who are worthy to participate in the blessing of Jairus's daughter. The rest of the multitude must wait outside. In this story, Jesus starts with "throngs" of people, but by the time He raises the girl from the dead, only six people are allowed to witness the miracle. When Jesus and His disciples enter the house, He immediately recognizes a general lack of faith. The noise in the household (see Matthew 9:23) does not lend itself to the administration of a priesthood blessing, so Jesus asks only the three apostles and Jairus and his wife to come back into the room with the "sleeping" daughter. The household of Jairus must have *believed* Jesus could heal, but when it appeared the girl was dead it became clear that most of them lacked actual *faith*. We must turn our belief into faith through action.

BE PATIENT

In my career as a therapist, I am expected to have endless amounts of patience, empathy, and a willingness to listen much more than I ever speak. For years I have gone to school, trained, and worked hard to be such a person. At times, I get overwhelmed and burdened with slogging through the "trenches," but most of the time I can remain present and focused for at least eight hours a day. At the end of the day, however, I tend to have little patience left. When I get home, I want to be heard instead of having to listen, and I want someone to show me a little empathy. I am ashamed to admit it, but sometimes I have very little patience or time for God to tell me anything. I am so busy pouring out my heart to Him and asking Him for direction in my life that I rarely find time to be still and listen. Throughout my life I have made plans, asked Heavenly Father to validate them, and then trudged ahead. This works pretty well until the Lord decides to change the plan. He whispers to me that I need to make certain changes, and I reluctantly do so, thus spiraling my carefully-put-together-life out of balance. As Jacob in the Old Testament did with an angel, the Spirit and I wrestle, and then we make a new plan.

I know God loves me. I know when He is silent it's not because He wants me to fail but because He wants me to come to Him. I know these things in my head, but in my heart I am often more like the man in the New Testament who says, "Lord, I believe, help thou mine unbelief" (Mark 9:24). I sometimes have patience, but not divine patience. I want to make things happen in my life, but somehow I lack the faith that moves mountains—the kind of faith to remember that God knows every hair on my head and every sparrow that falls. I call this kind of faith "expectation faith."

EXPECTATION FAITH

Expectation faith is about drawing upon the powers of heaven. You've most likely heard the phrase "The road to hell is paved with good intentions." Good intentions get you nowhere! Rex C. Reeve of the First Quorum of the Seventy said:

> *If we are going to draw upon the powers of heaven, intention is not enough. We must obey every word of command with exactness. Remember these words of the Lord: "I, the Lord, am bound when ye do what I say; but when ye do not what I say, ye have no promise" (D&C*

82:10). We must actually obey the law; intention is not enough. (Reeve, "Intention," 1981)

I love that promise from the Lord. He is bound. We can expect Him to fulfill His promises, but we must do our part and ask in faith. Elder Gene R. Cook declared:

Faithful Latter-day Saints will want to know how to use their faith to cause all things to work for their good (see D&C 90:24), to act and not to be acted upon (see 2 Ne. 2:13–14, 16, 26–27), and to righteously prevail over self and others and situations (see 3 Ne. 7:17–18). They will want to know the specific will of the Lord concerning themselves and then, in faith, discipline themselves to submit to His will . . . You too can literally cause things to work for your good both in your life and in the lives of others if you are full of faith in the Lord. "All things are possible to him that believeth" (Mark 9:23). Commit yourself in advance to what you righteously desire. The righteous exercising of faith will bring it about. (Cook, "Faith in the Lord," 1981)

Isn't that a powerful concept? Don't we all want to use our faith to make things happen in our lives? I think we all want to pull down the powers of heaven for our good. We simply need to find the balance between relying on the Lord and using the agency we fought for, to choose to do good things with our lives.

To earn money for my mission, I took a semester off school and worked full-time. When it came time to add up my money, I knew I had enough for my mission, and I remember feeling proud. However, I still needed to pay tithing, and if I did I would be short on paying for my mission. I struggle with plenty of gospel principles, but tithing isn't one of them. I knew that once I paid my tithing, things would work out. I paid my tithing, came up short, and asked my parents if they could make up the difference. Then came my farewell. Friends had made me an apron with handprints all over it. Throughout the day, cards and money were stuffed into the pockets of that apron. I didn't think much of it until a few days later when I was gathering up the money to take it to the bank. I was humbled when I counted the money and realized it was almost the exact amount I had paid in tithing. I had "expectation faith" that things would work out, and the Lord blessed me to be able to pay for my mission.

Another example of expectation faith relates to my trip to Ghana, West Africa. My sister was there doing research for her PhD, and I decided to go visit her. In preparation, I saved a lot of money, put together first-aid and mother's kits, got my shots, obtained my visa, and packed big suitcases full of things my sister had asked me to bring to her Ghanaian friends. I was excited to spend six weeks in Africa. Because I have severe allergies and a very weak immune system, I was nervous to spend such a long time in a foreign country. I had traveled abroad many times before, but had never stayed that long. I remember sitting on the floor of my living room, surrounded by all the clothes, kits, gifts, food, etc., that I was getting ready to pack into two giant suitcases, and feeling an overwhelming sense of joy. I had been planning and preparing to go to Africa for so long, and everything had finally come together. I pushed a few items out of my way and knelt down and poured out my heart to God. I asked him to keep me safe, protected, and healthy while in Ghana. I told Him that I had obeyed the Word of Wisdom all my life and I expected Him to keep His promise that I would be able to walk and not be weary, to run and not faint. I had never done anything like that before. It felt amazing, and the Spirit confirmed to me that I would be fine in Africa.

I arrived in Accra and was overcome by the heat. I listened to my sister about what foods to eat and how to eat them, what I could drink, and so forth. I absolutely loved Ghana. In the six weeks I was there, I never once got sick. I had no allergy problems, no diarrhea, no malaria—nothing. Even my sister was amazed. She'd had other visitors come, and all of them got sick. Every night I thanked the Lord for the amazing opportunities I was having in Ghana, but mostly I thanked Him for keeping His promise of health.

Elder Gene R. Cook said:

Expect the Lord to perform according to his holy will and your faith. His arm will be revealed. He will take care of his Saints. He wants other people to learn faith by your example. He wants you to cause things to happen. He wants you to draw upon his all-powerful arm and the power that resides in you to do things in his way. (Ibid)

There is no doubt in my mind that I stayed healthy in Africa because the Lord blessed me. I hope you look back in your life and find some experiences where you had expectation faith. I sometimes wonder what blessings I might be missing because of my lack of this kind of faith. I challenge you to find opportunities to prove the Lord. Find ways to increase your faith, to expect miracles, to expect the Lord to be bound to His promises. He is waiting to fulfill His end of deal—you just have to ask.

As quoted at the beginning of this chapter, Rainer Marie Rilke wrote:

> *Be patient with all that is unsolved in your heart and try to love the questions themselves as if they were locked rooms or books written in a foreign language. Do not now seek the answers, which cannot be given you because you would not be able to live them. And the point is, to live everything. Live the questions now. Perhaps you will then gradually, without noticing it, live along some distant day into the answer.*

This quote summarizes so eloquently how I often feel. The longer I am single, the more out of place I feel. I keep thinking the reason I don't seem to fit anywhere is because in the gospel scheme of things, I am supposed to be a mother raising children right now. Rilke reminds me to be patient with my heart, to let go of needing the answers now, but to love the questions. Doing this can be very difficult, but it is so freeing. I hope that as you've had a chance to read this book, your heart has been filled with questions. I hope you've been inspired by some of the principles that have blessed my life. I hope you will be a little more gentle with your heart and choose to live the questions in your life. When you do so, you will find unexpected joy.

Action Questions

- How can you practice believing in yourself?
- In what ways can you turn your belief and faith into action?
- How can you put the idea of "expectation faith" to work in your life?
- What are the questions of your heart?
- How can you "live the questions" in your life to the fullest?

SIXTEEN

Now What?

*Being single does not mean you have to put off being happy. As
President Harold B. Lee once said: "Happiness does not depend
on what happens outside of you, but on what happens inside of
you. It is measured by the spirit with which you meet the problems
of life" . . . My advice to those of you who are single is to pray
often because our Heavenly Father, who knows you best of all,
knows your talents and strengths as well as your weaknesses.
He has placed you here on the earth at this time to develop and
refine these characteristics. I promise you He will help you.
He is aware of your needs, and by and by those promised
blessings of companionship will come to you.*
—JAMES E. FAUST ("WELCOME," 2007)

At this point, you might be asking yourself, So now what? You
might be feeling a bit overwhelmed, excited, and overloaded
with a lot of information. You may be wondering where to
begin or how to apply the things you've learned.

When I was in the middle of finals for my last semester
of graduate school, I was completely overwhelmed. All
the different areas of my life—school, church, internship,
relationships, and so forth—seemed to be blending into each

other. I felt like a failure as a roommate, sister, friend, and coworker. It seemed as if all the boundaries I built to separate the areas of my life were crumbling. I needed help, so I called my dad. I asked him how he handled teaching part-time, going to school for his PhD, having a son die, being in the bishopric, being a husband, and being a father of eight kids, all at the same time. He told me, "You know how you eat an elephant? One bite at a time." I couldn't believe that was his advice and told him so, but that approach really was what had helped him survive. He told me to take one bite at a time, do one task at a time, and take one day at a time. About a year later, I sent him this text: "I need some guidance, Dad. I feel a bit lost in my life. Things aren't too bad—I just need a plan."

He called me and said I could move home into the extra bedroom. I laughed—which was much better than crying—because my dad seemed to know exactly what to say. I told him I couldn't move home because I was thirty-one and people just don't do that. He told me he figured I'd say that, but by his offering he knew I would realize things could be much worse in my life. He was right on both counts. I made it through grad school by taking one bite at a time, and I am making it through life by recognizing all the blessings in my life. So I offer you the same advice.

Now what? Now you eat the elephant one bite at a time, recognize your many blessings and the things you are doing well in your life, and apply the things in this book that have touched your heart. Don't try to do too many things at once. Let the Spirit guide you as you navigate through. Again, I issue the challenge of the title of this book, *Make It Happen.* What are you going to do with your single life? How are you going to build the kingdom in your own unique way? What are you going to contribute that no one else can or will? You may be single, but you can make amazing things happen in your life.

Action Questions

- Take time to journal, blog, write, or discuss some of the things that inspired you. Enjoy the feeling of validation—of knowing you are not alone.
- Who do you know that could benefit from the principles in this book?
- What other principles or lessons have you lived or learned in your life as an LDS single that inspired you to be happy and make things happen in your life?
- What are you going to do today to make things happen in your life?

Sources

Benson, Ezra Taft. "Jesus Christ: Gifts and Expectations." In *Ensign,* Dec. 1988.

Cook, Gene R. "Faith in the Lord Jesus Christ." In *Brigham Young University 1981–82 Speeches.* Provo, Utah: Brigham Young University, 1983.

Eyring, Henry B. "Spiritual Preparedness: Start Early and Be Steady." In *Ensign,* Oct. 2005.

Faust, James E. "Welcome Every Single One." First Presidency Message. In *Ensign,* Aug. 2007.

Fosdick, Henry Emerson. *Twelve Tests of Character.* New York: Harper & Brothers, 1923. 87–88.

Hinckley, Gordon B. "Forget Yourself." In *Speeches: Brigham Young University 1977.* Provo, Utah: Brigham Young University, 1978.

Holland, Jeffrey R. and Patricia T. *On Earth as It Is in Heaven.* Salt Lake City: Deseret Book Co., 1989. 69.

Hymns. Salt Lake City, Utah: The Church of Jesus Christ of Latter-day Saints, 1985.

Johnson, Robert A. *We: Understanding the Psychology of Romantic Love.* New York: Harper Collins Publishers, 1983.

Lewis, C. S. *The Four Loves.* New York: Harcourt, Inc., 1960.

———. *Mere Christianity.* New York: Macmillan, 1952.

———. *The Screwtape Letters.* New York: Macmillan, 1943.

Monson, Thomas S. "The Divine Gift of Gratitude." In *Ensign,* Nov. 2010. 87–90.

Nelson, Russell M. "Face the Future with Faith." In *Ensign,* May 2011.

Oaks, Dallin H. "Dating versus Hanging Out." Church Educational System broadcast from Oakland, California, May 1, 2005.

———. "Good, Better, Best." In *Ensign,* Nov. 2007.

Okazaki, Chieko N. *Aloha.* Salt Lake City, Utah: Deseret Book Co., 1995. 119.

———. *"Cat's Cradle of Kindness."* In *Ensign,* Apr. 1993.

Reeve, Rex C. "Intention Is Not Enough." In *New Era,* July 1981. 4.

Rilke, Rainer Marie. *Letters to a Young Poet.* New York: W. W. Norton & Company, Inc., 1934.

Secretary's Journal. Jan. 28, 1857. Quoted in Neal A. Maxwell, "Be of Good Cheer," *Ensign,* Oct. 1982.

Sill, Sterling W. *Leadership.* Salt Lake City, Utah: Bookcraft, Inc., 1958.

Strayer, Chelsea Shields. "I Love to See The Temple." Retrieved March 24, 2011 from http://www.the-exponent.com.

"A Sure Trumpet Sound: Quotations from President Lee." In *Ensign,*

Feb. 1974. 78.

Taylor, John. In *Journal of Discourses.* 26 vols. Salt Lake City, Utah: Deseret Book Co., 1884. 24:197.

Thomas, M. Catherine. *Spiritual Lightening.* Salt Lake City, Utah: Bookcraft, 1996. 55–56.

Wirthlin, Joseph B. "The Virtue of Kindness." In *Ensign*, May 2005. 26.

Wolpe, Rabbi David. *Making Loss Matter.* New York: The Berkley Publishing Group, 1999.

Young, Brigham. *Discourses of Brigham Young: Second President of The Church of Jesus Christ of Latter-day Saints.* Comp. John A. Widstoe. Salt Lake City, Utah: Deseret Book Co., 1925. 180.

About the Author

Kylee Shields works as a shadow (family therapist) at the ANASAZI Foundation and enjoys having the Tonto National Forest as her office. When she isn't writing or working, she loves to travel and play the piano. She loves trains, Avengers (Captain America), straws, arches, bridges, architectural stairs, drumming on her steering wheel, and singing out loud. Kylee is the co-founder and music director of INSPIRE, a musical fireside group. For more information about the principles in this book, please go to kyleeshields.com.